Indira Gandhi

A Biography

ELA SEN

PETER OWEN · LONDON

ISBN 0 7206 0063 6

634240
920 ,
20 - 3 . 74

PETER OWEN LIMITED
20 Holland Park Avenue London W11 3QU

First Commonwealth edition 1973
© Ela Sen 1973

Printed in Great Britain by
Daedalus Press
Stoke Ferry King's Lynn Norfolk

In Memory of

Alec

Contents

Illustrations

Frontispiece

Indira Gandhi

1   Indira Gandhi as a child, with her parents
    Jawaharlal and Kamala Nehru

2   Letter from Jawaharlal Nehru to the author

3   Indira Gandhi with her sons, Rajiv and Sanjoy

4   Indira Gandhi with her grandson, Rahul

The frontispiece and illustrations 1, 3 and 4 are reproduced by courtesy of
the Press Information Bureau, Government of India.

Foreword

It was as a young wife and mother that I first met Indira Gandhi through her aunt, Krishna Hutheesing, who was a close friend of mine. It was soon after Indira's eldest son Rajiv was born, at the height of the independence struggle. It was through Krishna that I became acquainted with most members of the Nehru family, although I had met Jawaharlal Nehru earlier in connection with a book I was then writing.

I was of that generation which, during the historic struggle for Indian independence, was inclined to look to Jawaharlal Nehru for all the answers to its questions. He had studied the changes that had swept through Europe from 1917 onwards. He was Mahatma Gandhi's 'window on the West'.

Jawaharlal Nehru used to be flooded with letters from people all over India, seeking his advice and offering their services in the cause of nationalism. He always replied to them. This habit he kept up even as Prime Minister, and his daughter, the present Prime Minister of India, is as approachable.

Once in the 'thirties, after a very successful passive resistance campaign had been called off by Mahatma Gandhi because violence had broken out, unable to understand that to Gandhi non-violence was real and dynamic, I wrote to Pandit Nehru a letter full of queries, certain that he would give me some explanation. He took the trouble to reply (see Plate 2).

Indira Gandhi has inherited a great many of her father's qualities including that of recognizing that within the masses lies

1

the strength of a nation and that they should not be ignored. She, too, replies to most letters sent to her, except those held up by petty officials.

In the years between, since 1947, I had made my home in England with my Scottish journalist husband, to whom the Nehrus had extended a friendliness and trust on his own account. So our contacts with them did not lapse, although these were dependent on their trips to London and ours to New Delhi.

In 1949, when Pandit Nehru was Prime Minister of India and was living in the old Commander-in-Chief's residence, which had become the Prime Minister's residence, he invited us to an informal dinner. I was suitably awed by the sumptuous luxury of the house and by the attendant, resplendent in livery, behind each guest's chair. Indira and her aunt Krishna were there; the dinner party was truly informal, with the Nehru charisma dominating the atmosphere.

I remembered the simplicity of the Nehrus in the past, the true simplicity of people who are used to the best and have experienced the worst.

Just before we left for England we had been to visit Indira and her father at 17, York Road, in New Delhi. Pandit Nehru was then Prime Minister of the interim Government. Indira was looking like a pale, transparent shadow, after the birth of her second son Sanjoy. A great deal was happening in their private lives but no outsider ever got a hint of this. Indira was reserved and serious, but when she smiled there was the hint of inward joy. Neither father nor daughter had learnt as yet to put on their public faces. They were naturally reticent about personal problems.

We met again in London in the year of Queen Elizabeth II's Coronation. Indira Gandhi can hardly be expected to remember that on Krishna's advice she rang me up on the telephone to ask a very womanly question – the name of a good hairdresser. She remains very feminine. Neither office nor power has changed her personal characteristics.

All the Nehrus have, apart from their undoubted charm, a

great quality of loyalty to their real friends. Indira is no exception, as I have discovered in the last five years. However busy, she has always found time to see me when I asked for an interview.

Indira Gandhi came to London the year after her father died. She was a member of the delegation to the Commonwealth Prime Ministers' Conference. Lal Bahadur Shastri was then Prime Minister of India. When I went to see her to convey my condolences personally, Indira was as poised and collected as ever, but her face showed her deep grief.

In the years since 1966 that Indira Gandhi has been Prime Minister, I have met her practically every year and watched her feeling of insecurity give way to one of complete confidence in her own powers to carry out her father's plans for moving India towards socialism. It was said at the beginning of her ministry that she was not aware of parliamentary procedures, that she would contradict herself, that she was inexperienced. People were anxious to see her fail, but they had counted without her courage and she was determined not to fail. She got little support from anybody except the unimportant people who came to her open home sessions each morning, and from her advisers. When I met her in 1966, I asked her if she was getting enough support. In her quiet manner she said : 'The Party chiefs don't like me, but the people of India do and they will support me.' She looked frail and as if she needed friends and somebody to see that she had regular meals, but then one has always felt this about Indira, forgetting how sensible she really is.

When Indira Gandhi came to London in 1968 for the Commonwealth Prime Ministers' Conference, I interviewed her for the *Times*. She gave me an appointment at a time when she thought she would be fairly free, but she was not. She rushed in from the Conference with the television cameras and lights having been set up in her sitting room in Claridge's. She called me in and I conducted my interview while she changed for dinner with the Wilsons. At that time she was tremendously interested in family planning (she still is) and she told her secretary to let me have such relevant figures as she had with her. It was then that she spoke of her son designing the 'people's car' for India – today the 'Mathurin', as it is called, is at the prototype stage.

Until her landslide victory in 1971, of which she had been quite confident, I saw her mostly informally in her home, sipping tea or, in the summer, drinking lychee juice squeezed from fresh lychees. Every time she appeared to be gaining more and more self-confidence and to be growing in stature. Gentle, kindly and unruffled as she had always been, one still felt that she needed friends everywhere.

I met Indira Gandhi in December 1972 after India's great victory on the Bangladesh issue over her enemies at home and abroad. Her reception was friendly, but this time I saw her in her office in Parliament House. There was a heated debate going on in Parliament as to how to curb the activities of the CIA. In her chambers we had a long talk for the purposes of this book. Her manners were impeccable and in deference to the difference in our ages, in memory perhaps of her aunt who was no more, Indira Gandhi stood up as I came into her room. It was good to see her looking as cheerful as she did and completely secure in herself. We spoke without inhibition, the subjects ranging from family matters to foreign policy.

This time, however, I felt I was speaking with a Prime Minister, who was quite sure of herself and of how to meet India's many problems.

I should like to thank Indira Gandhi for all the courtesy she has shown to me over many years and especially for allowing me to interview her for the purposes of this book.

Acknowledgements are due to Lord Mountbatten for permitting me to interview him and for talking to me about Indira Gandhi. Also to P. N. Hakser, Padmaja Naidu, Harry De Pennha, P. C. Chatterjee, Girilal Jain, K. D. Malviya, Shiva Ramakrishna for their support and help and to Air India who made possible my trip to India for the purpose of interviewing the Prime Minister.

May, 1973   *Ela Sen*

I

A Citizen of India

President Nixon has described Indira Gandhi as 'that cold blooded lady'. President Johnson said of her in 1966, when she went to the USA at his invitation during her first short period as Prime Minister of India: 'A very proud, very gracious and very able lady.' Mrs Lyndon Johnson, when she returned from India in 1961, remarked: 'To understand India you must have a teacher like Indira Gandhi; I was lucky in this.' Jacqueline Kennedy became a personal friend of Indira Gandhi and the Nehru family. These are four personal American assessments.

Earl Mountbatten of Burma remarks: 'I met Indira in 1947, as Mr Nehru's pretty, young daughter, rather reserved and aloof. Although I had no idea then as to what heights she was capable of reaching, I did sense a steel-like quality under the calm exterior.'

When Indira Gandhi became Prime Minister in 1966 for her first term, her aunt Vijayalakshmi Pandit remarked: 'My niece is frail of health and not strong enough to carry the duties of a Prime Minister.' Mrs Gandhi remarked to journalists who quoted her aunt to her: 'I am neither frail nor weak when it is my job to carry out tasks entrusted to me.'

Nijalingappa, the President of Congress O, as the isolated rump of the once monolithic Indian National Congress is called, just before the 1971 elections described Indira as 'an arrogant woman'.

The ordinary people of India, the poverty-stricken masses of

India, who make up 85 per cent of India's 550 million, speak of
her as '*devi*' – a goddess.

A foreign journalist, who enquired of one of the minority of
affluent Indians the best way of getting to the Prime Minister's
residence in New Delhi where he was to interview her, was told
sarcastically, 'The best way is to take a trishaw (a cycle rickshaw);
the driver will take you right to the main entrance and probably
won't even charge a fare. These are the sort of people who know
best how to get to her.'

Some British people are surprised to see political power entrusted to a woman : 'Who is the man behind Mrs Gandhi, surely
all these decisions are not her own?' She has advisers, she listens
to what they have to say. She is not an autocrat but, as one of her
principal advisers put it : 'Believe you me, the decisions are hers,
make no mistake about that.' One of her female critics grudgingly
said of Mrs Gandhi after the Fourteen Day War with Pakistan :
'We have always said India needs a dictator. We have got one
now, only it is a woman !' This was intended to be compliment-
ary, but it is doubtful if Indira Gandhi would consider it to be so.

There are some, among the rich minority, whose attitude
towards the Prime Minister is almost vicious, who are convinced
that the people's idol is not invulnerable and long for the day
when the image will topple, tarnished and discarded. There is no
political crime of which they are not prepared to accuse her.
Their greatest frustration at present is that she cares not for the
barking dogs who follow her caravan at a distance. Indira's
defensive mechanism is that she *believes* that what she is doing is
for the good of the largest number. She is intelligent enough to
realize what games unscrupulous politicians can play with an
illiterate mass of people, but she also believes in the innate
commonsense and ability of the Indian masses to understand who
and what benefits them most. Mahatma Gandhi used to say
'Love is never misplaced' and this is what one imagines would
sustain Indira at the most difficult times.

An Italian picture magazine has described her as 'Queen of
India'; this title too she does not want. She believes in democracy

that will lead to a socialistic state in India. Like her father, her desire is to let capitalism and socialism co-exist; no blood baths and no suffering even for the rich. But the little man's rights and opportunities have to be safeguarded. The rich, who have not been dispossessed, but whose vast profits have been cut, do not realize that Indira Gandhi is their safeguard against complete dispossession and even death.

Indira Gandhi's ancestors came from Kashmir about two hundred and fifty years ago – in the closing era of the Mogul rule. They were Brahmins. The earliest was a scholar of considerable standing, who greatly impressed one of the later Mogul emperors – Emperor Farukhsiyar – who asked him to come to Delhi to add lustre to his court. In 1719, Raj Kaul did so; the Emperor presented him with a house in Delhi and also gave him a cluster of villages to provide him with an income. The villages were along a canal or *nehra*. The family name was 'Kaul', which became 'Kaul-Nehra' or 'the Kauls who own the villages round the canal'. Ultimately, it was whittled down to Nehru. Raj Kaul could work at the court of a Muslim ruler, for there was so much freedom from religious intolerance that Hindus had no difficulty attaining important positions.

Mrs Gandhi's great-great-grandfather worked as a *vakil* or legal representative of the East India Company at the Mogul Court, because of the influence the family had. Her great-grandfather was the Chief of Police for Delhi for the last Mogul emperor.

The Nehru family, including Indira's grandfather Motilal, who was a mere boy then, went through troubled times following the revolt of Indian soldiers in 1857. They fled from Delhi to Agra, leaving their worldly possessions behind, where the older brothers carried on their legal practice and from where Motilal Nehru also qualified as a *vakil*. The British by this time were well established as rulers of India and they moved the High Court of the United Provinces (today called Uttar Pradesh) from Agra to Allahabad. Thus Allahabad became the home of the Nehrus.

Indira's grandfather was a brilliant lawyer, especially in the complicated Hindu laws of inheritance. When Jawaharlal Nehru was born, his father was a man of moderate means; but within ten years, by his own merits, he had become one of the foremost lawyers and one of the wealthiest men in Uttar Pradesh. His wealth continued to multiply until his meeting with Mohandas Karamchand Gandhi, when Indira was about three years old. What happened is now part of India's history.

The Nehrus were like any other opulent, middle class family in India. In Allahabad there were the Saprus, the Malaviyas, the Zutshis, the Kunzrus – all as well known as the Nehrus. The fact that the name has now a touch of magic and has become almost legendary is due to the high-powered personal qualities of, first, Motilal Nehru who built a practice that made him one of the richest men of his time, only to push it aside in the cause of nationalism; then Jawaharlal Nehru, who spent half his life in prison in the cause of India's freedom and became India's first Prime Minister; and now Indira Gandhi, the present Prime Minister of India – an outstanding woman to whose hands the people of India have entrusted full political power. Lord Mountbatten called her 'the most outstanding woman in the world today'.

After the Nehrus, many other Kashmiris also emigrated from Kashmir into northern India. Some settled in Uttar Pradesh, where they found their own friends and relations or just other Kashmiris who were there; like all *emigrés* they sought the familiar among the unknown. Today, these people, of whom Indira Gandhi is one, are part of India wherever they have settled. Most of them intermarry, although all the Nehru women were married out of the community. Kashmir remains a hereditary memory of their past history. They have little in common with present day Kashmiris, not even language.

Indira Gandhi's rise to power was far from spectacular or sudden; it was the result of sheer hard work. Circumstances and her father had given her a rigid training all her life. It could be compared in some aspects to the disciplined training of a future reigning monarch in countries that still retain a monarchy. The inculcation of a sense of responsibility, diligence and discipline was all the more difficult in Indira's case because her future was so uncertain. There were no prospects to visualize. India was still tied to Britain. When the time came, however, she was not found wanting, because all through her adult life she had been companion to her father, Jawaharlal Nehru, India's first Prime Minister. In the last ten years of his life she had been closely associated with him in his work, discussing problems and helping him when he needed help most.

Jawaharlal Nehru was often asked privately and publicly 'After Nehru – what?' He used to say, and he meant it, that in a country of 400 million people there were surely several persons capable of filling the job of Prime Minister. He never built up a line of would-be successors. When asked if he was grooming his daughter to take over after him, he had truthfully said : 'I would not like to appear to encourage some sort of dynastic arrangement. That would be wholly undemocratic and an undesirable thing.' Therefore Indira had no personal illusions or grandiose ideas of taking advantage of her father's following to contest the leadership of India. By nature she was withdrawn, introverted, even to the extent of aloofness. Brought up on politics, she had no desire to become a politician.

The Nehru women are all attractive, all vivacious and more than willing to be noticed in a crowd of people. They inevitably attracted a great deal of attention. They were like a flock of beautiful, chattering birds, sometimes rather ostentatiously dressed in silks and jewels. Indira exuded tremendous charm, with a tasteful simplicity of attire. Her father never liked her to flaunt jewellery. She hardly ever wore the beautiful jewels inherited from her mother. She spoke softly. She smiled often, but her gentle charm in her younger years was overshadowed by the vivacity and social chatter of her female relatives. Indira had no desire to compete with them. As someone once remarked : 'Indira is the only quiet member in a chattering family.' She could not chatter but she could always converse, and could hold the interest

of anybody who cared to spend time with her. She loved the
serenity and quietness that was in her father. They each knew
what was in the other and there was no need to underline anything. Indira's relatives were not, in those days, jealous of her.
The future was hidden. Not many of them realized that there was
a steel-like strength under the soft, non-competitive exterior.
When this emerged much later, it surprised her female relatives,
who felt that they were better and more experienced at the game
of manoeuvres than she was.

Although brought up on her father's beliefs in the Russian
Revolution and the theories of Marx and Lenin, the furthest
Indira ever went in her youth was to lean towards the Socialist
Party and keep her links with and belief in the British Labour
Party. Her father, Jawaharlal Nehru, was far to the left of her.
As she matured, she could have been described as a social democrat with Right Wing leanings. Her father's foreign policy of
non-alignment suited her. She had no reason to be anti-American
after her first visit to the USA, where her father was given a
ticker-tape reception. Her disillusionment with the USA began
perhaps with the Vietnam War and her reluctant admiration for
the Viet-Cong and the North Vietnamese, who were fighting so
stubbornly against such superior odds. She realized that the North
Vietnamese were an enduring people; that they deserved a stake
in their country.

The Congress Party President, Nijalingappa, remarked in 1969,
when Indira had been reinstalled as Prime Minister by popular
vote : 'She did not show all the socialism that she talks of now
when we made her Prime Minister in 1966.' This is fair comment.
But in that year, 1966, Indira had spent much time in trying to
find out the reason for Congress's loss of support in the country.
She had realized that this lay in its unkept promises to the people
of India; there had been no real economic improvement. She
realized that her father's idea of a socialist state meant the real
application of socialism. If she was to get back into power, she
must make the people realize that she was on their side. The
Congress had promised many reforms through the years, which

lay in resolution form in the Minutes, but nothing had been done. If the country was not to drift into communism, as it had been for the last few years, she must seek allies in the Socialist and Communist Parties and find the right advisers to help her to keep faith with the people.

The people, the so-called masses, reacted by believing in Indira Gandhi, by trusting her as they had trusted her father; thus, slowly, Indira Gandhi was impelled to move towards socialism. Between 1966 and 1970 Indira matured fast; she grew in stature and developed into a woman of great self-confidence. She saw her way clearly. In 1966, she had been overwhelmed by her reception in America, but it was the same person who in 1970 was able with firm courage to refuse to attend a dinner given by President Nixon. There had been a serious slip-up in protocol by the American Ambassador to India, who had failed to see Mrs Gandhi off at the airport on her departure for the USA; this was considered to be an insult. In four years Indira Gandhi had made herself a true representative of the people of India.

Indira Gandhi is now fifty-five years old. She has been elected Prime Minister twice, having previously served one year's 'apprenticeship' as Premier under very critical conditions. The enmity of her female relations has grown with her success. Some have spoken openly against her as Prime Minister; others have written words giving great comfort to her enemies. During the time she has occupied the foremost position in India, she has been absolutely free from nepotism. It has been said that Lord Mountbatten, whom she considers a family friend, once asked her to take her aunt Mrs Pandit into her Cabinet, but that Indira Gandhi very politely replied that she must make her own decisions. In 1970 Mrs Pandit gave up her seat in Parliament, bcause she did not approve of her niece's policies. Some other female parliamentarians have also shown a particular type of enmity towards her. Envy has been perhaps the main motive. Her enemies were all routed in the 1971 General Election.

Mrs Gandhi, after her overwhelming victory in 1971, has tried to recruit men and women of her own age group into the Cabinet, retaining only a few of the older and more loyal personalities. If there is a preponderance of persons of Kashmiri heritage among her ministers and advisers, this is the only criticism one can make. But in any case, their ability is unquestioned.

Indira has two sons, Rajiv and Sanjoy. She is a devoted mother and has always cared deeply for them, even after she and her husband separated. She has tried to bring them up as citizens of India with a proud heritage. It is to her credit that so long as her husband was alive, his sons always spent some time with him. She did not try to keep them apart or to allow parental differences to have any effect on the boys' relationship with their father.

Rajiv is now married to an Italian girl and they have two children. He has trained as a civil aviation pilot and works for the internal airline company, the Indian Airlines Corporation. His mother has not in any way used her influence to help either of her sons. Sanjoy has been trying to develop India's first small car, all the parts being made indigenously. Unfortunately the car monopoly lobby in Lok-Sabha has made it impossible for Sanjoy to obtain the licence required for manufacture. Indira has not smoothed his path at all. He has to fight his own way.

Both Indira's sons live at their mother's residence. Her Italian daughter-in-law appears to fit into the family *ménage* perfectly. Although Indira continues to live in the house allotted to her as Minister for Broadcasting and Information in 1964, she has been allowed the use of the adjacent house as well since her family has grown. This is her private home. Indira enjoys the role of a grandmother, and the home life which now surrounds her. It has brought great happiness to her.

Mrs Gandhi, without being domesticated, which her job does not permit, is involved in domesticity. She takes time off to discuss the day's engagements and menus with her social secretary. If she is free, she prefers to lunch with the family. This is her relaxation. Her taste in food is catholic and she is not fussy about what she eats. She receives the guests for her dinner parties in an elegant drawing room and, an accomplished hostess, remembers their preferences in food and drink. She oversees the flower arrangements in the rooms and ensures that the seating is correct at the dinner table.

Her study is furnished in an unobtrusively contemporary style, both functional and elegant. But there is another part of her residence which has rather old fashioned colonial-type furniture, where she talks to her Party members, the representatives for the various States and officials on brief business visits. It is like any government office, bleak and impersonal, in any part of India. The marked difference between the two parts of her residence is surprising until one realizes that this is how the people who go to see her expect to find their Prime Minister. The elegance would be strange to them, the other is familiar. The identification between her and the people is much more complete in surroundings which do not overawe.

A portrait of Indira's father dominates the drawing room. A few chosen antiques find place on the walls. The sitting room opens onto a green lawn with well kept borders and seasonal flowers. Indira is fond of gardening, but she can find little time for it these days, although she still supervises the management of her garden. Her politeness to people who work for her is unfailing. She likes to lead a quiet life whenever she can, but she also does not like to disappoint those people to whom her presence, either at a son's or daughter's wedding, would mean much.

Indira still manages to keep her 'open home' morning meetings for any member of the public who wants to go along. These meetings are not organized or used to build up her public image. She listens to grievances, complaints and problems. If a problem can be rectified, she passes it on to the Cabinet member or official responsible. Otherwise, having completed her enquiries, she explains to the complainant the reason why nothing can be done. This is one of the ways in which she keeps in touch with the people, who realize that her concern is not a facade, but is genuine.

Apart from her large office staff – officials, ministers, clerks – the Prime Minister has one private secretary at home and two at her office in the Secretariat. She also has two social secretaries, both women, at her residence, one of whom always accompanies her on her visits abroad. She is most particular that her home should be as properly and as efficiently run as her office. The social secretaries find that this is one of their main tasks.

Mrs Gandhi has no need to attract attention by wearing startling colours or jewellery. Flamboyancy is not in keeping with her character. She wears clothes which are compatible with her dignity and position and also with her age. Harmony is her keynote. Indira never looks as if she put on anything in a hurry; she gives the appearance of being totally relaxed. Her well-coiffured black hair looks all the better for the startling grey streak above the right brow. She has the flair to dress correctly for each occasion, in spite of the long day which is normal to her.

Indira Gandhi wakes at six in the morning, when the world around her is coolest and at its best in the morning sunshine. She does her yoga exercises, baths and breakfasts, and is ready to meet whoever attends her 'open house' for one hour. Now she sees her grandchildren, who bring a welcome interruption to her routine, before she goes to her office duties as Prime Minister in the South Block of the Secretariat, built by Sir Edward Lutyens in red sandstone for the British rulers of India. The steps of the stairway have been worn down by the feet of petitioners and officials with files in days past. Lifts were installed a long time ago and today visitors or officials do not have to trudge up and down the stairs, but the messengers and office boys still do so. The offices are built with green spaces on both sides and breezes blow through, keeping the inside moderately cool during the day. The South Block is occupied by the Prime Minister, members of her Cabinet, her advisers and the officials and clerks working with them.

From the office Mrs Gandhi goes to Lok-Sabha (the lower House of Parliament), when Parliament is sitting. Since she is also the Home Minister, she is present at question time to answer those questions which relate to both her portfolios. If affairs are critical there is often no time for lunch, but other days she goes home, where more often than not there is a house guest she is happy to meet and relax with; or there are foreign journalists and visitors who cannot be fitted in at any other time, so she sees them at lunch time and then it is very like work. She is happiest to be able to eat with her own family privately. After this short interlude she goes back to Lok-Sabha and her office. Much of the day and most of the evening is spent in attending public functions. Sometimes she is able to return home, to bath and change, but at other times it is a question of following her schedule of engagements punctually, and without a break.

There are occasions when the Prime Minister has to leave New Delhi for business in one of the States. She has been known to leave early in the morning by plane for Punjab, working continuously during her journey. Dressed simply but impeccably, she climbs into the waiting jeep, having accepted flowers and garlands. She is whisked to her meeting with crowds cheering her all the way. The wind blowing in her face, hair flying all the time, she smiles and waves. She addresses a large meeting of civilians and Party members. The army entertains the Prime Minister to lunch, at which she has to speak again. A helicopter takes her after lunch to meet the *jawans* (infantry men), to whom she talks and praises them for their part in the recent Indo-Pakistan War and their vigil on the borders of India and Pakistan. Indira Gandhi's plane takes her next to the neighbouring State of Haryana and she addresses a mass meeting there, returning to her residence in New Delhi at 9.30 p.m. This is not an unusual day for India's Prime Minister particularly if Parliament is not in session.

Mrs Gandhi is very much the hub of her Party and is always ready to help out the Chief Ministers of the States, if they have problems. They come from all over India to consult with her how best to carry out the tasks they are facing. She encourages them to come to her when they need her, as also the Party officials. The language she uses in talking to them is mostly Hindi, but to the non-Hindi speaking people of the eastern seaboard and the hill areas, she uses English. Unlike some of her countrymen, she is liberal in her views about language.

Indira Gandhi leads a working life, while remaining wholly feminine. She has an inner confidence which has remained unshaken by the enmity and discouragement that harassed her first year as Prime Minister. She has not lost faith in her own ability to do the job which the people of India have given her. She can be tough when necessary, but she can use her femininity when she feels this will get her what she wants more easily.

When Indira, after the 1967 elections, was reinstalled as Prime Minister, a foreign journalist asked her whether she had found it a handicap to be a woman in her present position. Indira Gandhi replied : 'If you say that this job is only for a man, that a man has certain qualities and capabilities that a woman does not have – then what are those qualities? Physical strength? No, if you are looking for weak points, you can find them in anybody and I don't think a person who is a head of state should think in terms of himself or herself as belonging to any group – whether in sex, religion or caste. If the people accept you as the leader of a nation, that is all that matters.'

Jawaharlal Nehru was an agnostic and he brought up his daughter as one too, leaving her, of course, the freedom to develop in whichever way she wanted, although she now says that her father read the Hindu *Bhagvad Geeta* every day. The *Geeta* contains sermons by Lord Krishna to Arjun, the Warrior, on the correct path to wisdom and life, similar to Buddha's teachings or Christ's Sermon on the Mount. In his own writings Nehru always said he was an agnostic and his daily reading of the *Geeta* does not prove the contrary. Indira does not believe in organized religion of any kind, but she is not an agnostic. She believes in the Hindu concept of a Supreme Intelligence directing all. Did the change occur when her father died? He had given her a feeling of security and his death robbed her of her anchor. It was, perhaps, the insecurity of her life and future which sent her in search of that Supreme Director of destinies, who might have the key. Indira Gandhi is a visitor to the *Ashram* at Pondicherry, where lives an aged French woman of ninety, to whom the practice of yoga is said to have given mystic powers. She is known as the 'Mother' and her blessing is thought to be powerful. Not many see the 'Mother' or obtain her benediction, but, according to disciples at the *Ashram*, Indira has received it.

Astrologers force their attention on Indira, as is their custom with the great and important. Coincidences in life are not uncommon, but Jawaharlal Nehru's scientifically-minded daughter has no time for them. She displays the realism and scientific efficiency on which she has built her life. Yet it is true that messengers from the 'Mother' flit between New Delhi and Pondicherry with advice and directives for the Prime Minister. Does she take heed of these words? If so, the advice given so far has been good.

2

Early Life

When Indira Gandhi was born, on 19 November, 1917, her grandmother said a little sadly : 'It's a girl!' Most mothers of that period hoped that their adored and only sons would have a boy child to inherit and carry on the name – as much in homes where they inherited nothing as in the lavish and sumptuous homes like that of the Nehrus. Indira's grandfather gently reproached his wife, saying : 'This daughter of Jawahar's [Pandit Nehru] may prove better than a thousand sons.' An aged tutor on his death bed, when shown the baby, said : 'May you illuminate the name of Nehru.'

The First World War was drawing to a close with Britain exhausted but victorious. In India, it was the start of the Gandhi era. A 'little old man' – even then this man from Gujarat, with his large protruding ears, and spectacles, seemed wise and therefore 'old' – was bringing new enthusiasm and fresh ideas into his age-old country. He was fresh from leading the oppressed Indians in South Africa in their struggle to obtain certain basic rights. Young Jawaharlal Nehru, newly returned after several years in England, was immensely attracted by his personality and his theories of non-violent non-co-operation as a means to achieve India's independence.

Thus, Indira Gandhi was born into an historic age, in which non-violent non-co-operation was to become not just a theory, but the weapon by which India was freed. It was a possibility difficult to believe in then.

18

The Nehrus were rich and lived sumptuously in a mansion, in a select neighbourhood of the country town of Allahabad. Grandfather Motilal was a lawyer – an advocate – qualified in India, as distinct from a barrister, which his son became. In the district courts, an advocate of exceptional calibre, as Motilal Nehru was, had every chance of building up a very large practice from the surrounding landlords, maharajahs and rich merchants. He enjoyed the European way of life and modelled his own on those of the leisured classes in England. He was an anglophile, who believed that the English always honoured their word. This was at the turn of the century. Twenty years later the wind of change was to roar through the mansion called Anand Bhawan, or 'the abode of joy'.

One of the spectacular events in the year 1916, in northern India, was the marriage of Jawaharlal Nehru to Kamala Kaul, whose father lived in Delhi and was an orthodox Hindu. Thus, Indira's mother, at the age of seventeen, was not a westernized girl, but this was easily remedied in the Nehru household. As soon as the engagement was announced, Motilal requested her father to let Kamala come and stay with the Nehrus to get to know their way of life before she became one of the family. The request was unorthodox and in 1916 was considered 'way out', but Jawaharlal Nehru, though merely a very handsome barrister then, was perhaps the most eligible bachelor among the Kashmiris. Therefore Kamala's father temporarily put aside his scruples to allow his daughter to visit her future in-laws and even to get acquainted with her future husband. This was of course carried out in a very Victorian manner with chaperons, but was nevertheless daring in that day and age.

Apart from her physical loveliness, Kamala's great recommendation for Motilal Nehru was that she was a very healthy and robust individual. His own wife had been a semi-invalid all their married life and he had cherished her like some precious and fragile piece of porcelain. For his son he wanted a healthy girl, able to bear children.

At the time of her marriage, Kamala was just a young girl, unacquainted with western ideas and ways, but she was intelligent, and very quickly realized what was expected of her. Furthermore, Motilal Nehru was a determined man who wanted to give his son the right sort of wife. Even after all his years in England, Jawaharlal Nehru made no attempt to assert his independence. He was confident that his father and mother knew his thoughts and ideas. He was prepared to fall in love with the girl of his parent's choice. So Kamala came and went as a visitor to what was to be her home.

Kamala was impressed and perhaps a little scared by the lavish home, which was soon to be hers. The Indian side of the household was something she understood, but the European side – the large drawing room, the large dining room, crystal chandeliers, priceless rugs and carpets, silver and glass – filled the young bride-to-be with awe at its splendour and its unfamiliarity.

The stables were full of horses and grooms for the young Nehrus, the kennels had dogs of various breeds and then there was the English governess, whose added duty was to instruct the bride-to-be in the ways and manners of English society. She was taught to speak English. Kamala was a good daughter, who obeyed her father and adhered to her future father-in-law's wishes. She learned her lessons fast.

But does anyone know what Kamala, at sixteen, really felt about this transplanting? She did not want to disappoint her father-in-law and she did not. She liked and admired her new sisters-in-law. Her future husband was like a fairy prince though, like most Indian brides-to-be, she only caught glimpses of him. Even in the same house, it was not possible to get to know him better until they were married. If there was a courtship, it was very Victorian. She was a proud girl and was confident that she could be the equal of her future relatives. Did she, perhaps, find refuge and comfort in her future mother-in-law's domain, which remained as Indian as was Kamala's home, away from the English atmosphere and splendour of the rest of the house? There are no records of those early days or of her reactions.

It was only years later that Kamala 'failed' her father-in-law, the apple of whose eye she had become since those early days. The girl chosen for her health and robustness developed tuberculosis. But much was to happen before that.

With utmost pomp – today it might be called ostentation – the marriage of Kamala Kaul and Jawaharlal Nehru was celebrated. It was as if the son of a king came to Delhi to marry his wife. The Nehrus and their relatives travelled by special train and set up camp, which was rather like the creation of a small town. The tents were hardly camp-like, they were more like houses, with an army of servants to attend to the needs of the guests. The bride wore floral jewellery, except for the traditional gold chain and bangles essential for a bride. The following day, on her arrival at the bridegroom's home, she would be ablaze with diamonds and jewels – gifts from her father-in-law.

The Nehru mansion in Allahabad had thirty-seven rooms and the young couple were given a suite of their own to set up home and be independent. But in the way of Indian families, for all their veneer of anglicization, the newly-weds lived mostly as part of the family.

Relationships between Kamala and her in-laws followed the usual pattern. Her father-in-law accepted her completely and she became very dear to him. Kamala had a sweet temperament and she knew what was due from her as a daughter-in-law, but she also had quite a strong will and it was inevitable that there should be some clashes with her mother-in-law, who made no secret about who was to dominate Anand Bhawan. Krishna, the younger sister-in-law, was a child of nine when Kamala came as a young bride and they became very close. This love Krishna transferred also to her young niece Indira.

Mrs Pandit – Swarup, as she was called then – slightly resented the newcomer, who had won all hearts in the household. It was a traditional sister-in-lawish rivalry; at the time of Kamala's marriage, she and Mrs Pandit were of the same age. Unfortunately, in later life this feeling of rivalry also dogged her niece Indira.

Jawaharlal and Kamala lived at Anand Bhawan extremely

happily and in 1917 their daughter Indira was born, a small, perfectly formed baby, with an abundance of curly black hair. She was light coloured, as are most Kashmiri Brahmins. The new addition seemed to complete the pride, joy and happiness of the Nehru family. Indira was born in her grandfather's home, which was later to be donated as a gift to the Congress Party.

The parents wanted to call their daughter Priyadarshini, or 'dear to behold', and as her father said in one of his letters from prison 'dearer still when sight is denied'; but the grandparents had decided on Indira. Indira is another name for Lakshmi, the goddess of wealth, but also in this case it was her great-grand-mother's name. So she was called Indira Priyadarshini and to all those who loved her or were close friends she was known by the diminutive 'Indu'.

The wind of change was already beginning to blow and Jawaharlal Nehru was getting restless. He was a student of Marx-ism and on his daughter's thirteenth birthday he was to write to her from prison that the year of her birth was 'one of the memor-able years of history, when a great leader with heart full of love and sympathy for the poor and suffering wrote for his people a noble and never-to-be-forgotten chapter of history. The very month in which you were born, Lenin started the great Revolu-tion, which has changed the face of Russia and Siberia. . . . In India today we are making history and you and I are fortunate to see this happening before our eyes and to take some part our-selves in this great drama. . . .'

Indira Gandhi spent her babyhood and childhood in the great mansion where she had been born, but even within two years of her birth there were great changes in the lives of the Nehrus, par-ticularly in that of her own father and mother. Indira saw little of the sumptuous splendour which had surrounded the youth of her father and her aunts.

Although unsophisticated and with a virginal look that cap-tivated Jawaharlal, Kamala was a girl with an obstinacy and wil-fulness that matched her husband's. She was sensitive, proud and impulsive. If Kamala actively disliked anybody, she seemed to recoil within herself and freeze; this quality her daughter appears to have inherited. But the characteristic was not obvious in Kamala because in the company of friends she was usually gay and bright. Although she had had no formal education like her husband, she had very definite views and liked to express them fearlessly, to the point of an embarrassing directness. Kamala was no dreamer or idealist like her young husband, but her realism added in no small measure to his strength.

In those early years, when Nehru was trying to take what was to him a momentous decision, which would inevitably mean repeated separation from Kamala and his daughter, as well as imprisonment and other consequences, she was sometimes very lonely, because he was so pre-occupied most of the time. She often felt alone in a houseful of new relatives who, however kind, were still formal. Her only consolation was her baby girl. Much later, after her death, Nehru wrote: 'She gave me strength, but she must have suffered and felt a little neglected. An unkindness to her would almost have been better than this semi-forgetful attitude.'

In their youth, both Kamala and Jawaharlal showed the same characteristics of wilfulness and quick temper and, like most young couples who love each other, they quarrelled frequently. Jawaharlal retained these qualities until he died, but illness mellowed Kamala. More than anything, she would have liked to participate in the initial struggles of the non-co-operation movement with her husband, but the baby still needed a mother's care, although she was dearly loved by her grandparents, aunts, uncles and cousins. Anand Bhawan was still a happy house, reverberating with many voices and filled with the personality of Motilal Nehru.

In 1919 Gandhi first injected revolutionary content into the Indian National Congress, which until his leadership had been little more than a debating society for British-educated intellectuals. It had been founded by an Englishman and a civil servant, A. O. Hume, and had become a private club for anglophiles who, in spite of their belief that India must be free, thought that freedom would come through the British.

At this period, when even the then far western world was shocked by the massacre at Jallian-Wallahbagh, just outside Lahore (Punjab), of people holding a peaceful nationalist mass meeting, Jawaharlal Nehru was in his late twenties. This event, and the subsequent humiliation inflicted on the prominent citizens of Lahore, shook him to the core. It lifted him out of his world to seek that of Gandhi.

Indira was about three years old when Gandhi came to Anand Bhawan for the first time. The great leader, who was to bring independence to India, came on no white charger, but stepped out of a dusty third-class carriage, dressed in a white loin cloth and with a *chaddar* (cotton shawl) over his bare shoulder, his body uncovered and a large watch dangling from his waist. This was his way of identifying himself with India's poverty-stricken millions. The Nehrus, father and son, met him with due respect and escorted him into their car and their opulent mansion. Gandhi took his surroundings as he took everything else, calmly, but his diet of fruit and goats' milk and his appearance did not change.

Anand Bhawan was to be home from home for Gandhi, and the Nehru family were to become as close to him as his own. But this was only the beginning of the deep changes which were to affect the Nehrus and the Nehru household.

During Gandhi's visit to Allahabad he held prayer meetings and explained his ideas of how to achieve independence for India through non-violent non-co-operation; how passive resistance could be dynamic and positive and how much bravery it required to face blows and guns without weapons. He said that the strength of the united peoples of India would be able to fight the might of British imperialism.

At the point of Gandhi's departure from Allahabad, Motilal Nehru said to him : 'You have taken my son, but I have a great law practice in the British courts. If you will permit me to continue it, I will pour great sums of the money I make into your movement. Your cause will profit far more than if I gave it up to follow you.' Gandhi replied : 'No, I don't want money. I want you and every member of your family.'

Gandhi was not only a politician and a statesman, his prayer meetings showed him to be a psycho-analyst as well. He knew the Indian people could never be separated from their religion. The prayer meetings drew a cross section of the people and by this means he expounded his unusual theory of passive resistance. Through prayer it took root.

Since his return from England, Jawaharlal had not been content with the life he saw ahead of him. A lawyer like his father, the son of a rich man, he was part of a westernized society where he could take his place with the best. But he was dissatisfied. Marx and Lenin had been his teachers. He knew what was happening in Russia and the question in his mind was what could he do for his country. The British administrators, the Governor of the Province, the judges of the High Court were all friends of his father; they were often entertained at his home. They held his father in high regard, but Jawaharlal was still not happy.

When Jawaharlal was in his late twenties he joined Gandhi's army of non-violent soldiers and never had any misgivings that he had made the wrong decision. His action coincided with the first five years of his married life, so of necessity Kamala was often alone with her baby daughter and since the child's birth Kamala's health had been far from robust.

With his beloved son in the forefront of the struggle, it was not long before Motilal Nehru made a gesture, characteristic of the magnificence of the man and the magnificence with which he had surrounded himself. In reply to Gandhi's request he gave up his law practice and also became a non-violent soldier. It is reported that the then Governor of the United Provinces, Sir Harcourt Butler, who was a great friend of the Nehrus, said a trifle mockingly: 'If you go to prison, remind me to send you a case of champagne,' thus emphasizing Motilal Nehru's sybaritic tastes and the unlikelihood of such an event. Butler was quite wrong.

Indira's memory of her grandfather, expressed years later: 'I admired my grandfather as a strong person and I loved the tremendous zest for life which he had and which my father also developed later on, but I was tremendously impressed with my grandfather's bigness – I don't mean physically but, you know, he seemed to embrace the whole world. I loved the way he laughed.' A child's impressions are usually revealing, as in children's drawings in which the father figure appears to dwarf even the surrounding countryside.

With the departure of Motilal Nehru into the Gandhian field of battle, the outward splendour of the Nehru family began to diminish, as if the splendid crystal chandeliers were being dimmed one by one. This was the childhood background of Indira Ghandi. Motilal Nehru having nullified his vast income with one stroke, the dearly prized, precious luxuries had to be sold. To give them the courage they required to sustain this new, austere life, silks and satins gave way to thick (and in those days of the first hand-spun cottons they *were* thick), white, hand-spun saris; these helped them to identify themselves with the average man, as well as to give an impetus to the cottage industries, enabling the peasant to earn a little more. Boycott of foreign goods of any kind resulted in a bonfire of all the English-made Savile Row suits, jackets, coats, belonging to her father and grandfather. The child Indira watched the blaze, sensing the sadness of the family, but a bonfire is also fun.

From this period Indira grew up watching the beautiful things in her grandfather's home disappear one by one. Very often, this was done in order to meet fines imposed on either her grandfather or father which, according to the rules of passive resistance, they had refused to pay. On one occasion, her aunt Krishna Nehru records, she saw a precious carpet worth ten times the amount of the fines being removed from beneath their feet and she flew at the police inspector crying : 'You can't take that away, it's from our home and belongs to my mother and father.' Indira was only four years old at that time, but her political education had begun with the prison sentences on her grandfather and father. During the trial she sat in court on her grandfather's knee.

In fact, from the year 1921 the talk in the Nehru home grew more political day by day. Motilal Nehru gave up the mansion they had occupied and it became the offices of the Indian

National Congress. It was then called Swaraj (Independence) Bhawan. The family stayed for several years until the smaller house was completed, which still carried the name Anand Bhawan. This is the house which in 1971 Indira Gandhi presented to the nation, in accordance with her father's Will.

Indira's father was more often in jail than at home. All around her, relatives and friends of the family were joining the passive resistance movement and going to prison. This included her mother and her aunts. Her childhood was thus a continual preparation for the final struggle for India's independence. She waited for letters from her father.

Indira never knew the carefree days of social gossip and practice in the art of conversation. Her childhood and girlhood witnessed heavy political discussions, punctuated by swoops and arrests by the police. In her case, the once rigid Victorian discipline for children was swept aside by her grandfather, who liked to show off his grandchild to all who came to the house. She listened and absorbed political talk and gossip, as children do any grown-up conversation. She was slowly being prepared for the life she was to lead. It was early training, but there were no breaks.

As an only child will, Indira Gandhi created her own amusement, her own games. She spent her days mostly alone. Like all little girls she played with dolls, but with a difference. Her game was political theatre. She dressed her dolls in simple peasant garments, each carrying the Congress tricolour, made of paper. They faced policemen with batons and tin soldiers in helmets. Then she would address them as she had seen Gandhi, or her father and grandfather, addressing volunteers. She had watched processions from the verandahs of Anand Bhawan; she had witnessed demonstrations. She told the army not to fear and to keep the flag flying, that they must go forward without being afraid of the might of their British rulers.

When Indira was about nine years old, she was seen standing with her arms outstretched and muttering to herself. She appeared to be persuading an audience. She looked very solemn and her black eyes were ablaze. On being asked what she was doing, she replied: 'I am practising being Joan of Arc. I have just been reading about her and some day I am going to lead my people to freedom, just as Joan of Arc did.' It was all very real to her, watching people all around her prepared to suffer and sacrifice in the cause of India's independence. She too wanted to prepare herself, though she little knew what would be required of her forty years later.

During the intervals between prison sentences, when her father came back, Indira would sit on his knee, hold his hand and ask him to explain to her what was happening in his world. It was a difficult question to answer satisfactorily to a nine year old, but her father always tried to give a truthful and logical answer.

In the lonely house in which she lived, her grandmother was her refuge. She would pamper Indira, love her and give her the sweet things dear to all children. Her grandfather, when he was out of prison, was her friend, guide and philosopher. Even in his busiest moments he was never too busy for his granddaughter's whys and hows. All the time she longed to be old enough to be a real 'soldier in the service of India', as her father wanted her to be.

When Indira was in her early teens, she saw the whole family except her grandmother taken to prison. She applied to join the Congress Volunteers also, but was told that she was not old enough. So she decided to collect all the children in the neighbourhood and create her own army of volunteers, who could in small ways help those who were old enough to join in. There were surely jobs that they could do, she thought. She drilled them and disciplined them and they were used by the Congress to carry messages from one group of volunteers to another. They supplied quite a useful intelligence unit. Indira in later years described the work of the Monkey Army, as she called her brigade of boys and girls: 'Nobody bothered about an urchin hopping in and out of the police lines. Nobody thought that they could be doing anything. The boy would memorize the message and go then to the people concerned and say: "You know this is what has to be done or not done. All the police are there. So and so is going to be arrested," or whatever the news was. In other ways we also acted as an intelligence unit, because frequently the policemen sitting in front of the police station would talk about what was going on – who was to be arrested, where there was to be a raid and so on, and four or five children playing hop-scotch outside would attract no one's attention and they would deliver the news to the people in the movement.'

In prison her grandfather heard of the Monkey Army and wrote to her: 'What is your position in the Monkey Army? I suggest the wearing of a tail by every member, the length of which should be in proportion to the rank of the wearer. The badge with the print of "Hanuman" [the Monkey God] is all right, but see that the *gada* [club], which is normally in Hanuman's right hand is not there. Remember that the *gada* means violence and we are a non-violent army. Have you got someone to teach you marching and drilling? It is essential. Above all you have to keep yourself fit. *Papu* [her father] runs two miles every morning. You ought to be able to run at least one mile without stopping and increase the distance gradually. . . .'

Those who today express surprise at Indira's competent leadership as Prime Minister and assert that she had never shown promise before, should follow her early life from the day she started to train herself to be Joan of Arc.

After Indira's birth, Kamala's recovery took unusually long and she would grow tired very easily. This weakness persisted and after she gave birth to a son, who did not survive, she became more or less an invalid, but an invalid who refused to take her illness seriously. In the end it became clear that Kamala had tuberculosis, extremely prevalent in India at that time. Doctors said that a spell in Switzerland might effect a cure. So in 1926 the little family of three set off together for Switzerland, where later on they were joined by grandfather and Aunt Krishna. Kamala's real cure, many people felt, would be effected by the presence of her husband and child and the rare moments of happiness now allotted to them.

Indira was then nine and started going to school, which pleased her father, who was worried about her education; her first steps in French were learnt there. She went to the Ecole Nouvelle in Bex in the mountains, where she also learnt to skate and ski. Brought up on politics for food and drink, she found it very odd that her schoolmates knew nothing about politics. Their interests seemed to lie all in sport.

Kamala's health, however, did not improve in Geneva, so she was moved to a better sanatorium at Montana Vernala. The excellent treatment at this sanatorium had quick results and she felt well enough gradually to travel around with her husband, always taking Indira with them.

Though a child, Indira did not find adult conversation between her father and the famous men he met boring or un-interesting – she was enthralled. The little girl sat absorbed through an intellectual discussion between her father and Romain Rolland. She enjoyed meeting the famous German poet Ernst Toller. She also accompanied her parents to the celebrations for the tenth anniversary of the October Revolution in Moscow. Her father had been invited to attend the occasion. Friendship with Russia thus began quite early in her life through her father.

Kamala's health had improved greatly and the Nehrus went back to India and the independence struggle in February, 1928.

New Year's Day, 1931, should have meant hope and happi-ness, but for Indira, little more than thirteen years old, it darkened into greater loneliness – her mother was arrested. Her father wrote that he had been thinking of her and her mother on New Year's Day when he heard news of Kamala's arrest : 'I have no doubt that Mummy is thoroughly happy and contented, but you must be rather lonely. Once a fortnight you may see Mummy and once a fortnight you may see me and you will carry our messages to each other. But I will sit down with pen and paper and I shall think of you and then you will silently come to me and we shall talk of many things. And we shall dream of the past and find our way to make the future greater than the past.'

In some ways, during the twenty-six years which her father

spent in gaol, Indira was luckier than many other children who have their parents with them, because he thought constantly of her. Every letter he wrote to her in prison contained the message expressed in his letter quoted above. This sentiment formed the basis of his letters to her, in which he taught her the value of science and the appreciation of culture and history. Through them ran the silken thread of hope for the future and the hope of being with his wife and child again. For a lonely little girl, these letters were her treasure house. They laid the foundation of the closeness which was to bind them all their lives. They also taught her that frontiers of countries are usually man made. Each man or woman inherits the traditions of the earth on which we all live. There is no monopoly of the past.

In some of his letters, Jawaharlal Nehru commented on his own people, comments both objective and perceptive which added to Indira's storehouse of wisdom received from her father. 'Another tendency to be noticed in India is the desire to look back and not forward; to the heights we have occupied and not to the heights we hope to occupy. And so our people sighed for the past and instead of getting a move on, obeyed anyone who chose to order them about. Ultimately empires must rest not so much on the strength as on the servility of the people over whom they dominate.' Somebody once in conversation with Jawaharlal Nehru in pre-independence days preceded his statement with 'When India becomes great. . .' He got no further; Jawaharlal Nehru interrupted with the remark : 'India *is* Great.' This was his firm belief and his sufferings seemed worthwhile in that context. To Indira he gave this faith too.

The death of Motilal Nehru in February, 1931, struck the first note of tragedy in the Nehru family. His son and daughter-in-law were released from prison to be by his bedside. He had been a *paterfamilias* in the old tradition. Now the family stood alone. Jawaharlal was far too politically involved to take on the sturdy responsibilities required of the head of the family. Her grandfather's death left a blank in Indira's already lonesome life.

Kamala's health was again showing signs of a breakdown and

Jawaharlal now took his wife and daughter for a sea voyage to
Ceylon. Kamala was inconsolable at the prospect of having to
abandon her political work, but this holiday with her husband
and daughter did much to boost her health.

Indira's formal schooling had been causing a great deal of
worry to Jawaharlal and he had been giving much thought to it.
The days of resident governesses and tutors were over. She had
to go to a suitable school, but preferably within reach of where
he himself or her mother and aunts might be gaoled, for he knew
his freedom would be short-lived. Matching all these conditions
seemed impossible. Indira was not robust enough to be able to
take a rigorous school discipline. On Gandhi's advice she was
sent to a school in Poona called the Pupil's Own School, which
was run by a Mr and Mrs Vakil. The Pandit girls were also sent
there. It was quite close to Yeravda goal, where at the time
Gandhi was imprisoned.

Indira took a few months to settle into school life. The company of her cousins helped and like most children anywhere in
the world, she adjusted herself and did good work while she was
there. She was diligent and conscientious, but the pain of separation from her parents was always with her. While she was in the
Poona school, Gandhi undertook a fast unto death. Indira and
her cousins went to see him in prison. This scene they all knew;
it was familiar to them.

Indira went to a large number of schools, trying to keep up
with her parents' wishes as well as their whereabouts. Her very
first school had been St Cecilia's Convent, run by nuns in
Allahabad; she was sent there as a day girl by her grandfather,
but Gandhi disapproved of her education in a foreign school and
she was taken away from there, although her father had no real
objections. Later she was sent to school in the mountain resort of
Mussoorie, because her father was in Dehra Dun gaol, in the
plains very close to Mussoorie. During the holidays, she would
come back to the family home in Allahabad. It would be lonely
unless her mother or cousins were there. But from childhood
Indira had learnt the art of living with herself.

From prison, where Indira's father was serving a two year sentence, he wrote regularly to her, trying to supplement her education with lessons in history and its application to present times. Kamala's health had not improved and at the time of his release in 1930, she was under treatment in Calcutta. Nehru took Indira with him to be reunited with his wife.

Jawaharlal had a great admiration for the poet Tagore, who had established a university in a village near Calcutta and called it Santiniketan, which has since become world famous. Nehru liked its unorthodox approach, the co-education and the emphasis on the arts and languages. He enrolled Indira as a student and left her there while he and Kamala returned to Allahabad. She had already passed her matriculation examination. However, after only one year, where she learnt a great deal about the appreciation of art and poetry, Indira left Santiniketan, because her mother's condition had grown worse. Tagore himself wrote to her father : 'I have watched her very closely and have felt admiration for the way in which you have brought her up. Her teachers all in one voice praise her and I know she is very popular with the students.'

After this, life was to take many twists and turns for Indira. At the age of eighteen she accompanied her sick mother to Germany, fully aware of how very ill she was. Prior to their departure, her father was offered release from prison on condition that he gave an undertaking to cease his political activity. He was also allowed to come and see his sick wife for a day before she left. From her sick bed Kamala said : 'What is this about an undertaking? Do not give it.' Her health was failing, but not her courage. Kamala was admitted to the Badenweiler Sanatorium in the Black Forest in Germany.

While Kamala was at the sanatorium, a young Parsi, Feroze Gandhi, came into Indira's life. He was also from Allahabad and had joined the cause in the early days of non-violent non-co-operation. He was impressed by Kamala and her courage, and had become devoted to her. When he heard she had gone to Europe for treatment, he persuaded his rich aunt to send him there for further studies. Feroze came to Badenweiler and through his devotion to her mother, Indira grew to depend on him.

Towards the end of 1935, Jawaharlal was able to join his family in Germany. The last six months of his sentence had been suspended. For five months, Kamala, Indira and Jawaharlal were very happy, so much so that Kamala took a turn for the better and spoke of leaving Germany. They went to Lausanne and Indira went back to the school at Bex, where she had been once before, quite close to Lausanne. But the spirit and energy Kamala had shown burnt down slowly like a candle and on 26 February, 1936 real sorrow struck Indira when her mother died.

Indira was now a young woman and the tragedy hit her hard, making her withdraw more into herself, except with her father, in whose brain beat constantly the words: 'Kamala is no more; Kamala is no more.' He took his daughter away for a few weeks to comfort and solace her – it was good for both of them to share their grief. It did not change anything, it did not lessen it, but it made them cling a little more to each other.

After her father's return to India, Indira went back for a short term to the school at Bex. Her father was keen that she should go to Oxford and she had therefore to get her London Matriculation before she could do so. She went to England, matriculated from Badminton School and then entered Somerville College, Oxford, to read English. At this time Feroze Gandhi had also come to England from Switzerland and had joined the London School of Economics. Always reserved and aloof, missing her mother and father and the hectic political life of India, for Indira Feroze became a natural companion. He was a familiar in a world of unfamiliars.

India, her father and what he was doing there were always with Indira and she used to go to London and work for the India League run by Krishna Menon, later to become India's first High Commissioner in London. Her father had established committees for aid to Spain and China and Indira worked to raise funds for these organizations. Hitler's armies were marching through Europe and she found great hope for India in the feelings of the young men and women in England who were flinging themselves into the International Brigade to help the Spanish Republicans. At this period she met La Pasiorana, actress and Spanish revolutionary leader. Her father's contacts in England were socialists and his admiration for the Spanish Republicans fighting fascism was tremendous. Indira shared all these feelings.

The writer Edward Thompson met Indira at Oxford and, being a friend of her father, wrote to him : 'I have seen Indu. She looks well and she is well. Sho looks thin, of course, and there is no doubt that just now she is what used to be called "delicate" and will have to go carefully. But she is wiry underneath and when she is past these difficult days of adolescence, she will pull into real strength.' How true the last sentence has turned out to be.

Christine Toller, the wife of Ernst Toller the German poet, said of Indira : 'She seems to be like a little flower, which the wind blows away easily, but I think she is not afraid of the wind.'

In the summer of 1938, Jawaharlal, temporarily out of gaol, went to Spain to see for himself what was happening. Then he went to London to collect his daughter for a tour of Europe. They were shocked at what Hitlerism had done to Europe – the tragic plight of the Jews, the Czechs and the Poles. In November Jawaharlal took Indira back with him to India until April 1939, when she returned to Oxford.

Indira enjoyed the years at Oxford. She liked the course she was taking and she liked her associates and professors. In 1940, however, she developed pleurisy and the fear of having inherited her mother's complaint haunted her. From her London hospital it was advised she go to Switzerland. But in Europe the 'phoney' war had finished and the real struggle was about to begin. Jawaharlal Nehru wanted to have his daughter back rather than leave her stranded in Switzerland for the duration of what had all the appearances of being a long war. Nevertheless, Indira went to Switzerland and was forced to remain there for almost a year. She was not able to finish her course at Oxford. She was certainly much better in health and the noises of war, though

close at hand, made Switzerland safer than Oxford. In 1941 she
returned to India to take her place in the independence struggle.
Her father was happy to have her back.

During Indira's return journey on a troopship via the Cape,
her ship stopped at Durban for a week. When it was known that
she was on the ship, the large community of Indians resident there
took her off the boat and she was able to see a great deal of the
sad state in which the African and Indian people of South Africa
lived. Indira advised Indians to identify themselves with the
Africans to whom the country belonged. She criticized the
Indians for their servility to their white rulers. Afraid of what else
she might say, the Indians avoided Indira for the rest of the time
the ship was in Durban.

Indira's return to Anand Bhawan was a dismal affair. The
house was a mere shell of its previous self. During her absence her
grandmother had died. So the loneliness was even greater than
what she experienced as a child. The long corridors, rooms and
verandahs had seemed empty and lonely to her as a child, but at
one end of it there had always been her grandmother. Indira felt
quite solitary when she returned from Europe. Jawaharlal was in
prison in Dehra Dun, so she rented a cottage in Mussoorie, so that
she could go to see him often and easily. Looking wan and frail
and feeling rather weak, she settled in at Mussoorie to recoup her
strength. Her father insisted on a proper medical check as soon as
she felt up to it. In the meantime, Indira brooded over her own
personal future. She was now over twenty-one and she felt pretty
sure that the next step for her would be marriage. She also knew
whom she wanted to marry – Feroze Gandhi. Feroze was somewhat older than herself, but perhaps she felt that the marriage
would mean security, of which she had known so little. A person
who had shown such devotion towards her mother and then been
such a constant companion to her in London would take away
the loneliness and solitude of her childhood. The continuity of her
relationship with Feroze had been brought about through her
mother, whom Feroze had devotedly admired and served as and

when he could; but during his first acquaintance with Kamala there had been no thought of marriage with her child Indira.

On one of her visits to her father in prison, Indira told him that she wanted to marry Feroze Gandhi. It was a shock to him and he reacted as most fathers would. He tried to dissuade her: Feroze was older than she, he came from an entirely different sort of people; his background, family and education were as unlike her own as possible. Religion had never mattered much to Jawaharlal, but now he pointed out even that difference – Feroze was a Parsi and the Nehrus were Hindu. None of his arguments were valid to Indira; she loved Feroze and she wanted to marry him. Jawaharlal Nehru implored her to wait a little, meet a few more young men and then make up her mind. Indira said that she had met quite a lot of nice young Indians in England, but her mind was made up about Feroze. It has to be said in all fairness that Feroze's family, not as illustrious as the Nehrus, but orthodox Parsis, had no taste for mixed marriages. They were as keenly opposed to the marriage as the Nehrus. Indira really had nobody to consult whose judgement she trusted. She missed her mother as never before. Kamala, she knew, had also understood and valued Feroze. She sought the advice of her aunts. Even her aunt Krishna, who was closest to her, could not help.

Indira's obstinacy and determination left no choice for her father and to quieten the public clamour against such a mixed marriage, he issued a statement: 'A marriage is a personal and domestic matter, affecting chiefly the two parties concerned and their families. . . . I have long held the view that, though parents should advise in the matter, the choice and ultimate decision must be with the two parties concerned.'

Indira was married at Anand Bhawan, Allahabad, in March 1942 to the man of her choice. Both she and her father hated ostentation and wanted a simple affair, but Ghandi advised that it should not be too quiet, lest the general interpretation should be that he had not approved the match. Thus, there were guests from all over India. The wedding was held in the open air under a canopy, March being an equable month, and was performed according to *Vedic* rites, which is the simplest form a Hindu marriage can take.

Indira's bridal sari was pale pink *Khadi* with tiny silver stars embroidered on it. The yarn had been spun by her father during one of his prison sentences. She wore only ornaments made of flowers, as her mother had done. Beside her father's chair was an empty seat with a jewelled cushion – it was the only touch of sorrow and remembrance for 'Kamala who is no more', but so dear to the three principal participants.

Her father, now a lonelier man than ever, was never far from Indira's mind. Even during her short honeymoon in the mountains of Kashmir, she kept thinking of her father in the heat of the plains and wrote: 'Wish we could send you some cool breezes from here.' He wrote back: 'Thanks, but you have no *mangoes*!' He too remembered how Indira loved that fruit.

3

Feroze Gandhi

Feroze Gandhi was a positive personality, who could not fail to make an impact on Indira. Chelapathi Rau, Editor of the *National Herald*, published from Lucknow, had said: 'I knew Feroze, fresh from London, with a bagful of enthusiasms, including enthusiasms for the Soviet Union and for machines. . . . The first person who had known his qualities of persistence and courage and charm had been Indira.' Indira, too, needed those qualities of determination and courage in order to marry Feroze Gandhi in the face of opposition from her entire family. To them, Feroze was simply not good enough for Indira. He came from a family with a modest background; Feroze's father's profession is nowhere recorded. Indira, however, even then recognized real values; she loved Feroze and was happy to start life with him in whatever capacity he could offer her.

People who knew her husband in those days say that Feroze was a friendly and intelligent man. His love for Indira had a protective quality of kindness and devotion which gave her the sense of security she needed, perhaps more than other girls of twenty-one. From within her he brought forth the sense of determination and resistance which a young girl needs if she is to do what she wants to do, in spite of the opposition of a well-knit family. Her father, Jawaharlal Nehru, behaved like the average parent in being greatly upset at her resolve to marry Feroze Gandhi. She knew her mother would have understood. If only for one reason, Indira should today be grateful to the man she married, in that

39

he brought her sterner qualities to the forefront. In the last few years, these have been among her greatest assets in withstanding pressures that could have weakened a less resilient person.

Feroze belonged to the Parsi community, whose ancestors had fled Muslim persecution in Persia in the eighth century and found refuge on the western shores of India. Othodox Parsis are fire worshippers and they worship the sun as the source of all life and energy. They are an extremely closed community, wishing to keep their hereditary strains as pure as possible. Therefore it required quite as much courage for Feroze to flout his family's opinions and feelings as it did for Indira to resist her family, only in her case she had also to take into account the nation's opinions. By this time Jawaharlal Nehru, Indians felt, belonged to them and the marriage of his daughter was of great public importance and interest.

After their honeymoon in Kashmir, Indira and Feroze returned to Allahabad. Both their families lived there. Feroze took a small house; they did not live in Anand Bhawan. Feroze, apparently, was a good handyman and he designed all the furniture for their new home. He was also a keen gardener and looked after their small garden meticulously. They were as happy as any newly-weds could possibly be. This was early in 1941.

The independence struggle was still strong and both Feroze and Indira became involved in it, as was inevitable. They were active workers for the Congress. Shortly after their return to Allahabad, Jawaharlal Nehru was arrested and sent to prison and in the following September both Feroze and Indira were arrested. Indira's world of security had once again collapsed. She accepted this as necessary. She was proud that she and her husband were playing their part in the national struggle, but life was harder than ever. This was Indira's first experience of gaol. However, in December 1941, just before the Japanese attack on Pearl Harbour, the British decided to release seven thousand political prisoners, among whom was Jawaharlal Nehru; his daughter, sister and son-in-law had been released earlier. Britain felt another bid should be made to get the people of the sub-continent on the allied side. The attempt was too half-hearted to achieve anything. Sir Stafford Cripps was sent by Churchill with proposals that gave nothing which could be interpreted as Independent Status; his mission was a failure. Gandhi, who until then had not wanted to embarrass Britain, agreed to Nehru's 'Quit India' policy and addressing the British he said : 'You have sat too long here for any good you have been doing. Depart and let us have done with you.'

On 7 August, 1942 a 'Quit India' resolution was put through the All India Congress Committee Meeting in Bombay by Jawaharlal; the resolution made it quite clear that this was not a threat, nor did it mean the withdrawal of British armies or nationals, but the withdrawal of Britons from political power. If this was done, the Congress agreed to form a provisional government which would give complete support to the allies. They could count on all-India support if the position was thus clarified. The result was absolutely the opposite of what had been planned : all Congress leaders were immediately arrested and sent to unstated destinations, thus silencing the only moderating voices that could influence the people. What had happened in Bombay was happening all over India. The people in a state of bewilderment, thinking their leaders had possibly been deported, raised the 'Quit India' banner in earnest.

After Nehru's arrest in Bombay one August morning in 1942, Indira and Feroze, with their aunt Krishna, followed the cars carrying the prisoners up to the Victoria Terminus railway station, but cordons of police stopped them going any further. All they saw were the prisoners being hustled onto the station platform, heavily guarded.

Indira went back to Allahabad with her husband. Life was even more difficult for those involved in the movement, which flared up in some places into acts of violence, a situation which would never have arisen if the voices of non-violence had not been silenced. Gandhi used to say that for him non-violence and passive resistance were matters of belief and principle, but for the mass of his followers they were politics and expediency. Mass

meetings, in fact all public meetings, were banned. Feroze had
gone underground and to Indira's anxiety about her father was
added worry for her husband's safety and welfare.

1942-45 were difficult years for the independence movement.
There was panic in the country, and rumours and fears about the
whereabouts of the leaders increased. It was necessary to stop
these rumours and only Indira could do this, because she was in
touch with her father. The situation between Congress and Government was more tense than it had ever been. The Government
decreed that it was illegal even to fly a Congress flag, but students
everywhere insisted on holding meetings to hoist the flag over
their college buildings. The students in Allahabad invited Indira
for the ceremony. As she arrived, she saw the police beating up
students with long batons and saw the boy with the flag fall to
the ground bleeding. She ran forward, took the flag out of his
hand and held it aloft. The police charged her and hit her across
the back and on her hands. At night, on the day she had faced
the baton charge by the police, her husband came secretly to see
her. He found her spirits undaunted. A few days later she was
arrested.

Indira was put in Naini prison, where Mrs Pandit had already
been sent; her daughter was also there, having been arrested for
taking part in a demonstration. While in prison Indira celebrated
her twenty-fifth birthday on the day she had her fortnightly interview with her husband, also in prison. Mrs Pandit wrote in her
diary: 'She came back looking very happy.' While in prison
Indira occupied herself by helping her cousin with her French,
which she had perfected during her various visits to Europe. She
and her cousin amused Mrs Pandit in the dreary, long evenings
by reading and acting plays. The three Nehru women remained
cheerful, in spite of the hardships they had to endure. Even such
a small event as a cat having kittens was a diversion.

At the time of her arrest Indira had been suffering from a slight
but persistent temperature. This continued to affect her while she
was in prison. Afraid that her condition might be deteriorating,
Government authorities released her on 15 May, 1943, together

with Mrs Pandit and her daughter. Mrs Pandit was re-arrested, but Indira had a bad attack of influenza, so she was left all alone. Afraid for his daughter's health, Jawaharlal begged her to avoid the heat in Allahabad and go to the cooler climate of a hill-side resort. She did so and remained there until Feroze was released in August, when they both returned to their home in Allahabad. Indira was able to resume her married life, which had been so rudely interrupted.

At the end of World War II all political prisoners were released and a Cabinet Mission, headed by Lord Pethwick Lawrence, came out to India to discuss the partition of India as part of a package deal for independence. The Mission failed as the Congress leaders refused to consider the partition of India. After the General Election in Britain in 1945, at which the Labour Party won a landslide victory and Clement Attlee was appointed Prime Minister, Lord Mountbatten was prevailed upon to go to India as Viceroy with the offer of independence, but with the formation of an independent State of Pakistan as the price of freedom.

In the meantime, an interim government was formed in 1946 headed by Pandit Nehru with an equal number of Hindu and Muslim ministers.

Feroze and Indira were then living in Lucknow, where Feroze worked as Manager of the daily *National Herald*, with which Jawaharlal Nehru was closely connected. They had taken a small cottage and transported all their furniture from Allahabad. Their home attracted a nucleus of intelligent and politically minded young people who enjoyed each other's company and served as stimuli for each other's ideas and aspirations. Indira and Feroze were foils for each other. She was reserved, shy and unforthcoming, but never inhospitable or uninterested. Feroze was an extrovert, jovial and informal. He also had an eye for a pretty face. Indira was involved in creating understanding and a loving bond between herself and her husband. There was a third member of the family now, who required a great deal of care and attention – this was their son Rajiv, who was born on 20 August, 1944 in Bombay, while Indira's father was still in prison. On

hearing the news he wrote from there: 'The birth of a new
member of the family always makes one feel reminiscent and
remember one's childhood days and other births. . . . Nature goes
on repeating itself, there is no end to its infinite variety and every
spring is resurrection, every new birth a new beginning, especially
when the new birth is intimately connected with us, it becomes a
revival of ourselves and our old hopes centre round it.'

Two years later, while Jawaharlal Nehru was heading the
interim government, Indira's second son Sanjoy was born in
Delhi. She had a much more difficult time than she had had with
Rajiv. Her British doctor, having tried to boss the Nehrus (always
a difficult task), finally claimed to have saved her life. To people
who visited her soon after the baby was born, including her
husband, Indira looked as if she had been pulled back from the
shadows.

It was now 1947 and while Feroze and Indira continued to
live in their backwater in Lucknow, Delhi was humming with
activity. The Mountbattens had arrived and the package deal of
freedom, but with the division of the sub-continent into India
and Pakistan, had almost gone through. The date for the transfer
of power was fixed as 15 August, 1947. News of massacres and
destitution saddened people all over India. The formation of
Pakistan, carved out of India, was a bitter pill to swallow. But
the alternative could be a civil war and worse carnage than was
already taking place. So the Mountbatten offer was accepted.

Indira frequently used to travel 176 miles between Lucknow
and Delhi to see that her father was comfortable and that all was
well with him. She would take her children with her and then
return to Lucknow to see that all was well with Feroze. When, at
Lord Mountbatten's suggestion, Pandit Nehru moved into the
mansion which had been the residence of the Commander-in-
Chief, it was imperative that Indira should go to help settle him
in in these new surroundings. It was then that Feroze suggested
that she should stop the strain of commuting between Lucknow
and Delhi and instead take their children and go to live in Delhi.
He would do the commuting. It was also at this time, after par-

tition, that Pandit Nehru started receiving threatening letters and Feroze realized that Indira's mind would be much more at rest if she were in Delhi with him.

After partition, there was retaliation for each blow struck at refugees fleeing from Pakistan or at Hindus who could not get away. Revenge and fear stalked Muslims in city after city in India. They lived in terror and prayer. Delhi was no exception. The Government and voluntary organizations all pulled together to stop this senseless killing. Indira, even though still not fully recovered from childbirth, also plunged into relief work. Nobody, least of all Indira, could stand by and watch innocents lose their lives. She was completely unafraid; this was perhaps her greatest danger, but she was certain even then that the people of India would not harm her.

Therefore, when Indira heard of a poor Muslim family in Old Delhi threatened with destruction, she went there in her jeep without an escort. Crowds with weapons were surrounding this tiny dwelling in the poorest slum. Indira walked through them; nobody lifted a finger against her, although the crowd shouted abuse. She found the inhabitants cowering in the darkest and furthest corner of their hut. Indira shepherded them out and into her jeep. The intended victims were not touched, neither was Indira, although jeers and cries of abuse followed her as the jeep drove rapidly out of reach of the crowd.

This incident was only one of many but, together with Lady Mountbatten, she continued to work for the resettlement of refugees and to deal with all the problems involved in tracing families and reuniting them. Never afraid of any situation, she tried to stop killings and save lives. It was a nightmare situation and men and women worked desperately to restore normality and sanity.

Feroze Gandhi's and Indira's political beliefs stemmed from intense nationalism and dedication to the cause of India's freedom. As has been mentioned earlier, it was Kamala Nehru, Indira's mother, whose courage and faith had inspired Feroze to become a soldier for India's freedom. For most thinking people in

India, independence and freedom was the immediate goal. After 1947, people were bound to diverge according to what they felt would be the best way to develop India. The Indian National Congress had embraced all nationalists within its fold – socialists, communists, Hindus, Muslims, Sikhs – under the leadership of Gandhi. Jawaharlal Nehru was somewhere between the socialists, mostly the younger generation, and the communists, including the young intellectuals, many of whom had graduated from British universities. The Labour Party of Great Britain was considered a good model for the rest of the Congress Party.

Indira and Feroze were close to the young socialists and remained so for a long time. In fact Feroze remained a Social Democrat, a position parallel with the Right Wing of the British Labour Party. He disliked communists and communism and what he described as their adventurism. His attitude was that of the *petit bourgeois*. His parliamentary career was thus based firmly on home politics, dedicated to making the air of India fit for the heroes of the national struggle to breathe. Foreign affairs and policy were not his direct interest. He wanted to get rid of corruption in high places, regardless of stature or class. He was clever enough to realize that the Prime Minister was well above all this and did not recognize it when he saw it, even in his own government officials.

In the 1952 General Election, Feroze stood as a Congress candidate for Rae Bareilly in Uttar Pradesh. He won by a large majority, gave up his position on the *National Herald* and went to Delhi to join his wife and children, where the Gandhi family occupied a suite in the Prime Minister's house. As a Member of Parliament he would have to spend most of his time in Delhi. People said that Feroze did not much like living at the Prime Minister's residence and resented being introduced as the Prime Minister's son-in-law. He much preferred the small house with a garden, which had been allotted to him as an MP. He took his work as an MP seriously and felt that much of his work might be embarrassing to his father-in-law, and that he might even be accused of having access to papers that he should not have seen.

Indira had now to choose whether to forsake her ageing father or to give up her private life with her husband; whichever decision she took, she would forever be haunted by the one she did not take. She would not leave her father. He needed her now. He had never failed her when she needed him. It is difficult for an occidental to appreciate the bond not only of love but of duty that ties parent and child in India and other oriental countries. It is invisible, nothing is ever said if the child fails, but its strength is immeasurable. Over and above all sense of duty, Indira loved her father dearly. At the crossroads one must have both vision and courage. Indira has handled her life with both.

There were some who said to Feroze that Indira preferred the limelight as the Prime Minister's daughter to her status as the wife of an individual. In spite of such remarks, Indira made her home with her father. He needed her, not only to care for his creature comforts, but to discuss and consult over difficult problems of state. Feroze understood this. Indira hated people to say that her marriage had broken down, because it was not true. She felt that there was real understanding between herself and Feroze, and both knew that her father needed her then as never before.

In a frank interview with an American woman journalist in Washington, in 1966, Indira said with some impatience : 'There is so much talk about my marriage having broken down. Our marriage was going through a difficult patch as most marriages do, but it had certainly not broken down.'

If there had been a breakdown, for their sons, at least, Feroze and Indira certainly kept their marriage as normal as possible, even while maintaining separate residences. Neither of them, whatever their own differences, would ever have created a situation that would adversely affect their children. They therefore developed their own solution to the situation, which was readily interpreted by those who wanted to do so as a break-up of their marriage. In fact, despite the gossip which inevitably surrounded them as public figures at the time, it is probable that their mutual decision represented a complete understanding which was the highest peak of their married life.

Pandit Nehru treated his son-in-law with affection. His grandsons brought great happiness into his busy life. He had wanted a
son, but he had never felt the lack of one, since Indira filled the
gap as well as any son could, perhaps better, with her woman's
intuition, understanding and sensitivity. Nevertheless, he watched
his grandsons with pride and pleasure as they frolicked on the
lawns of the Prime Minister's residence. He was physically
extremely fit and could enjoy childish games with them. Watching him made Indira's choice worthwhile to her.

Feroze initially stayed on at the Prime Minister's residence
with his wife and children, but used his house as an office, where
all kinds of people, who found the security in the Prime Minister's
house difficult to penetrate, could come to see him if they needed
his help. It was only after his re-election in 1957 that he actually
began to live in his MP's residence. He still came to the Prime
Minister's house for meals with his wife and children. He was an
extremely popular MP and took great interest in affairs for the
public good. Through his contacts, he was able to uncover in
Parliament two cases of gross abuse of public confidence.

The first concerned the misuse of funds by a life insurance
company, the Bharat Insurance Company, which belonged to
the powerful Jain Dalmia business complex. Feroze prepared his
case carefully, obtaining the precise facts and, in his first speech
before Parliament, placed them before the Lok-Sabha. A Commission of Inquiry was instituted and the Chairman of Jain
Dalmia and Bharat Insurance, Ram Krishna Dalmia, was found
guilty of unlawful business transactions and committed to prison.
This affair finally led to the nationalization of the life insurance
industry.

A second affair in which Feroze was prominent also concerned
life insurance. This time it involved the Government and was of
considerable embarrassment to Pandit Nehru. Neither was it easy
for Feroze. Public opinion said that he was deliberately trying to
discredit the Prime Minister. There is no reason to believe this; in
fact, his action performed a service for the Government of India.

The new case involved Government officials, and resulted in the resignation of the Finance Minister, T. T. Krishna-Maclain. This time a large loan from the nationalized Life Insurance Corporation had been irregularly sanctioned for Harides Mundhra, an influential business man. Feroze brought irrefutable proof to support his allegations against the Finance Ministry. A Court of Inquiry was held, with Feroze as the chief witness. As the facts were revealed, the case became more and more embarrassing for the Prime Minister, since his officials were involved. But Jawaharlal Nehru called for their dismissal and Harides Mundhra went to prison.

These were two cases for which the people of India will always remain grateful to Feroze Gandhi.

Feroze continued his parliamentary career as a champion of the weak and oppressed. He devoted all his energies to the fight against corruption in high places, feeling keenly that his task was to tear away the mask of rectitude from the face of corruption. He now lived in his own house, gaining great pleasure from the cultivation of his garden. During school holidays his sons, Rajiv and Sanjoy, spent a great deal of time with him. Feroze employed his skill as a craftsman in making mechanical toys for his sons. He enjoyed showing them how the toys worked and, of course, the boys were delighted. They enjoyed the happy moments they spent with their father, and Indira neither resented nor prevented their visits. She saw no reason to complicate the lives of her sons. She wanted them to have security and to grow up as balanced personalities. The boys loved both parents equally. The fact that they were never forced to choose between them helped.

Indira and Feroze were now launched on their separate careers; he as a parliamentarian, she more and more involved in Congress Party affairs and social welfare work, besides her role as consultant, companion and hostess to her father. Originally, differences between the young couple had started to manifest themselves over the question of careers. Although Indian women have never been curbed by men in the search for careers, Feroze felt the age-old sentiment that his wife had plenty to do at home with him and the boys. Yet he knew it would be wrong for him to become the centre of Indira's universe; she was so serious, so intense; she must turn to things outside the home also.

Indira was anxious to reconcile both sides of her life. Feroze, equally, wanted his fulfilment to be achieved independently of the Nehrus. Once they realized that these conflicting aims could not be reconciled, they decided to pursue their destinies separately.

Shortly after he had moved into the new house allocated to him as an MP in 1957, Feroze suffered a heart attack. Indira was in Nepal on a political mission, but rushed back on receiving the news. She nursed her husband right through his illness and then they went with their two sons for a restful holiday in Kashmir. Feroze returned happy, relaxed and well. Indira said : 'We had a nearly perfect holiday.' Feroze had his second and fatal heart seizure on 8 September, 1960, while Indira was in Kerala in the south, trying as Congress President to settle dissentions. As soon as she heard the news, she came to Feroze's bedside. Pandit Nehru muttered miserably to those near him while he waited for her return : 'He keeps on asking for Indu all the time.' Indira sat with Feroze for the few hours that were left. He died the next morning holding her hand, his sons by his bedside.

People have given Indira much pain by alleging that Feroze was not faithful to Indira in his married life. But she knew that their affection was mutual. Circumstances, the period in Indian history when they were born and a sense of dedication had forced them apart, as these had initially brought them together. Feroze had made his mark in public life as he had wanted to do, and this was shown by the numbers who attended his funeral. His mourners were not only the poor, or only the rich; they were from all classes – all came. Pandit Nehru commented : 'I never knew he was so popular, so loved.'

The final and real tribute Indira has paid to Feroze is that, while many of her relatives use either as prefix or suffix the well-known name 'Nehru', proud as she is of her birth and her father, Indira has made herself world famous as 'Indira Gandhi'. It shows loyalty to her husband and the name she took when she married him.

4

Life with Father

When Jawaharlal Nehru became Prime Minister on 15 August, 1947, Lord Mountbatten, still Viceroy of India, persuaded Jawaharlal to use as his residence the palatial building which had been occupied by the Commander in Chief, during the days of the British Raj. In independent India there was to be no Commander in Chief. The overall authority was to be divided between the Defence Minister, the Commander of Army Staff, the Commander of Air Force Staff and the Commander of Naval Staff. The residence, last occupied by Field Marshal Auchinleck, was more appropriate for the Prime Minister, who would be number two to the President. So from 17, York Road, where Jawaharlal Nehru had lived quite happily since he had become interim Prime Minister in 1946, he moved into the new Prime Minister's residence. Indira, who had been commuting between Lucknow and Delhi to see that her father's needs were not neglected, continued to do so, settling him in his new home.

Lord Mountbatten pointed out to Nehru that he would now have to play host to internationally eminent guests and that he would be able to provide in his new residence more office space for himself and his staff, which he badly needed. These arguments had their effect, although if it had not been suggested to Nehru that he change residences, he might quite happily have turned the official residence into some sort of museum and stayed on in his smaller home. The reality of his public duties, once defined, became apparent to him. but it is doubtful whether. at the start of an exciting new era for India, Nehru would have realized alone the importance of fitting the residence to the tasks ahead.

Jawaharlal Nehru was devoted to his two sisters, he loved his nieces, but as Frank Moraes, journalist and author, wrote in 1956 : 'The light of his eye, of course, was Indira, who now acts as her father's chatelaine at the Prime Minister's residence in New Delhi.' Many were astonished at the firmness with which Indira took up her position, making it quite clear that she was not prepared to relinquish it to anybody. This was a tremendous setback to the ambitions of her female relatives, who had been hoping that one or other of them would occupy that position. They had felt that even a fond and devoted father must recognize the superiority of their social talents to that of his daughter. He would sooner or later realize that she was not going to be a success as hostess, as entertainer of her father's world famous visitors.

Indira never excluded any of her relatives from social functions at the Prime Minister's residence. She tried not to let any of them feel unwanted, as she knew that would hurt her father. The family came and visited as guests and they were welcomed. But she never left anybody with illusions as to who was mistress of her father's house. People who would have presumed came up against that band of steel under the soft, unassuming exterior. If her father was ever aware of what was going on, which is doubtful, he must have been amused at his non-politician daughter's deft handling of family politics. Her able deflection and deflation of other people's ambitions was worthy of the best exponents of the art of politics. Later in her political life, she would know how to deal with those who thought they would be able to manoeuvre her out of office.

Early in this period, no sooner had the jubilation of independence died down than the lives of all Indians, and the Nehrus in particular, were shattered by the assassination of Gandhi on 30 January, 1948. The sound of that bullet reverberated throughout the world. For Pandit Nehru it was tragic; he was overcome, and he said : 'The light has gone out of our lives.' Indira's shock and sorrow were no less, but she had to try to help her father to steer out of the gloom that now filled his life at the death of his gentle, dearly loved, non-violent leader. Now there would be no voice to restrain people from political violence. That job had fallen to Pandit Nehru and his colleagues, ironing out all old differences.

Indira travelled abroad with her father on most of his visits to Europe, Asia, Africa and America. Among the first was a visit to the USA in 1949. Pandit Nehru was invited by President Truman and was given the famous ticker-tape reception. Indira felt some cynicism when she learnt that the next visitor who would receive a similar welcome was the Shah of Iran. It was feared in India that after the lavish reception Nehru had experienced in America, his socialist principles might be in danger. Public memory did not recall that in pre-independence days, American Democratic senators had upheld India's right to freedom. Jawaharlal Nehru, who had greatly admired President Franklin Roosevelt, had not forgotten this, nor the visit to India of Senator Lyndon B. Johnson, later to become President of the USA. Jawaharlal Nehru's socialism was deeprooted and unlikely to waver. Indira was apparently impressed by American hospitality and kindness; the honours heaped on her father and on herself as his daughter could obviously not fail to move her. One suspects, however, that she reserved one corner of her judgement for future developments.

Indira came to Britain several times with her father for the Commonwealth Prime Ministers' Conferences. There was a memorable one in 1949, when Pandit Nehru put forward the idea that India should become a Sovereign Republic within the Commonwealth and that the position of the Crown should be as head of the Commonwealth. The manner in which this was discussed and worked out is a tribute to Clement Attlee and his Labour Government and to Pandit Nehru's diplomacy. On 26 January, 1950, India became a Sovereign Republic, owing no allegiance to the British monarch, but recognizing him as the symbol and head of a free association of independent nations.

The next occasion on which Indira accompanied her father to Britain was in 1953, as a guest at the coronation of Queen

Elizabeth II. The ceremony at Westminster Abbey, the pomp and pageantry and the milling crowds in the streets, craning for a glimpse of their young Queen and her Consort, were memorable in every way. One of Indira's most interesting experiences on that occasion was her meeting with Sir Winston Churchill, who had once made so many adverse comments about India. The lion was ageing and he opened the conversation with Indira: 'Isn't it strange that we should be talking as friends, when we hated each other such a short while ago.' 'But Sir Winston, we didn't hate you,' said Indira politely – he was old and one must not be rude to old people. But he turned on her and said: 'But I did, I did,' and then added: 'But I don't now.' She also recalls that on the same occasion Churchill referred to her father as 'the man who has conquered hatred and fear.' A tribute indeed.

On her return from London, Indira was invited to visit the Soviet Union in a private capacity. This too was a valuable experience, for she had the opportunity to see life as it was in that country and to gain some knowledge of Soviet governmental machinery. She made a considerable impression on the Russian people. Many young mothers, as a compliment to her, named their newborn girls 'Indira'. It was an opportunity to acquire first-hand knowledge that was to be of use to her later on.

The following year Indira accompanied her father on an official visit to China, so she was able to compare the potentials of the two communist countries and their different approaches to communism. Her father invited Premier Chou En-lai of China to visit India, to discuss definite plans for friendship between the two nations, who had lived in peace for centuries. But Indira was not complacent and she spoke privately of her fears regarding China's intentions towards India and south-east Asia.

Indira accompanied her father to the Afro-Asian Conference at Bandung in Indonesia and, listening to the debates, she acquired some knowledge of the aspirations, fears and problems of the African peoples. She had also been with her father the previous year in Paris, where he addressed the United Nations General Assembly on India's foreign policy of non-alignment and the aspirations of the Afro-Asian peoples. Indira's education in foreign affairs was progressing fast.

In this way, gathering impressions of international affairs, she became a valuable counsellor for her father. Many of his old colleagues had died and those that were left spoke a different political language. His daughter understood, but she also argued the points on which they disagreed, as in the case of China. Over the border question, long before fighting flared up, Indira felt that a compromise agreement could be reached with China over the arbitrary MacMahon border line. The areas concerned were barren mountains to which the shepherds on both sides had access to graze their sheep for a couple of months only in the summer. The possession of appropriate parts of this area was no loss or gain to anybody. It was not worth breeding enmity over it. Her father believed that the Chinese would never adopt a policy of aggression and his Cabinet went along with this belief and suggested that he adopt delaying tactics. His colleagues were delighted when the Chinese proved him wrong, for this was what they wanted – Nehru had to learn that he was not infallible.

When Indira started going abroad with her father and later on had to travel all over India as Congress Party President, she had to make some arrangements so that the routine in the life of her sons should not be disturbed. They were still at a kindergarten school in Delhi. Indira asked a Danish woman, Anna, to take on the task of looking after her sons. This Anna did until the boys went to preparatory school in Dehra Dun. Then she took over more and more of the responsibilities for household chores from Indira.

Apa Pant, High Commissioner for India in London from 1969-72, commented : 'Pandit Nehru influenced his daughter, he moulded her mind from childhood, but very few people realize how greatly she influenced him.' He had known the Nehrus from the 'thirties and on a personal level. He also commented on Indira Gandhi's courage, quoting an instance when, as Indian Ambassador to Nepal, Sikkim and Bhutan, he accommpanied Pandit Nehru and his daughter on an official visit to Bhutan. Those were the days before the highways capable of carrying motor cars had been built: the only way of crossing the high Himalayan mountain passes was on horses, born and bred in Bhutan. The King of Bhutan produced fairly docile horses for his guests, although they were good horsemen. However, Indira noticed one spirited pony which kept throwing its groom every time he tried to mount. After watching its exploits for a while, Indira asked for permission to ride that pony. The Prime Minister of Bhutan asked the Indian Ambassador to try to dissuade her. Indira was not being foolhardy, nor was she trying something she could not accomplish. Fearing for her safety, the Bhutanese Prime Minister allowed her to ride the recalcitrant horse. She, however, easily quietened the horse and rode it up the mountain pass. Perhaps her freedom from fear calmed the horse's nerves.

Chou En-lai visited India in 1954 and all India turned out to greet him with the slogan 'Indians and Chinese are brothers.' Indira witnessed the confirmation of her father's great hopes of peace in Asia when the friendship of the two big Asian powers was ratified in the *Panch Shila* or Five Principles of Good Behaviour, which was signed by Pandit Nehru and Chou En-lai on behalf of their countries. Indira realized how happy this had made her father and saw that he would never be persuaded to doubt the good faith of the Chinese. But she knew how demoralized he would be if anything should go wrong. Dialogues about the border issue were in progress and the Chinese Prime Minister, while anxious that this one point in dispute should be cleared up, nevertheless showed no impatience.

Among the notable visitors to whom Indira played hostess were Bulganin and Khruschev, who also received a tumultous welcome in India. The visit came at the height of Khruschev's de-Stalinization days; his jovial character and statesmanlike approach to Indian politics made him an acceptable person in government circles. His introduction of de-Stalinization to the Communists of India was the initial cause of divisions in the party and the beginning of militant Maoism. But the Russians were shrewd enough to predict who would rule India for a long time to come and they cemented their relationship with Pandit Nehru and his Government. By this, Communism was weakened in India.

Jacqueline Kennedy was also a guest at the Prime Minister's residence when she visited India. Mrs Kennedy's popularity was undoubted – she was a glamour figure in India. She did more for the USA's public relations than did any hard-worked press attaché.

Lady Mountbatten was a regular 'cold weather visitor' to the Nehru household and was regarded almost as one of the family. She used to visit India on her way to other parts of Asia in the course of her work for the St John Ambulance Brigade. Indira, in her own quiet way, welcomed her; she knew that her father enjoyed Lady Mountbatten's company. 'My wife liked Indira,' says Lord Mountbatten.

Indira took her duties as hostess seriously and fulfilled these as well as the most accomplished society hostess. She presided over formal dinners with complete self-confidence; she moved among the guests at the Prime Minister's Garden Party as if she had done it all her life. She remained reserved and quiet, but left nothing undone. She treated all visitors alike. At the same time, she saw to it that neither her sons' nor her father's needs were in any way neglected. Rajiv and Sanjoy, with her father, remained the first concern of her life.

To the Prime Minister's residence came formal guests, guests whom the Nehrus liked having to stay and guests whom they were obliged to receive simply because they came to visit the Prime Minister of India. Indira welcomed all with unfailing hospitality and quiet confidence. Among those whom Pandit Nehru liked to see, even at breakfast if they could get up early enough for it, was Chelapathi Rau, who describes the scene : 'At breakfast and lunch and dinner, I was to see her [Indira] as a hostess, though for so unobtrusive and informal a guest as me, Jawaharlal Nehru, a host in himself, looked after much. . . . I was for some years a vegetarian, when Jawaharlal Nehru would seek to persuade me to help myself at least to fish and then I became a non-vegetarian. . . . Once Jawaharlal Nehru, taking rather an unusually personal view, suggested I was beginning to look a non-vegetarian. Indira would watch the operations of her father and the behaviour of the guests stoically, occasionally offering some help. The father was active, getting ahead, hectically serving himself with porridge or cutting *papaya* and distributing pieces, and nobody could cut fruit with the grace and artistry with which he could. . . . And beside the Rodin figure of the great man sat the daughter, nibbling at her food. . . .'

President Tito of Yugoslavia visited Pandit Nehru at the end of 1954 and for the first time Indira sat in on their consultations about future relations and the neutrality which both countries believed it was possible to maintain. From that time she was always present at her father's dialogues with other heads of state or Prime Ministers. Since she attended all such meetings and was fully aware of the international situation, it was easier for Pandit Nehru to consult her when he had something on his mind. In the same year, with President Tito as a witness to it, the Congress Party, at its annual conference, took the resolution which was to remain a resolution in the Minutes until Indira Gandhi as Prime Minister started to translate it into reality. This was that the Congress Party accepted 'a socialist pattern of society' for India's future development. Of all international figures, President Tito and then Nasser of Egypt, came closest to Nehru in appreciating what he was trying to do.

As the years went by, Anna took over more and more of the household chores from Indira, so that she could cope with the hectic life of international, high-level discussions and consultations with figures ranging from Chou En-lai and the Dalai and Panchen Lamas, to King Ibn Saud of Saudi Arabia and the Shah of Iran. Indira, during this time, was also a member of the Congress Working Committee, the National Welfare Board, a director of the *National Herald*, and a trustee of the Kamala Nehru Hospital. These and whatever other duties she accepted, she accomplished with all seriousness.

Chelapathi Rau, Editor of the *National Herald,* mentions that, young as Indira was then and although she attended few of the

Board Meetings of the *National Herald*, when she was asked to
handle a situation she would arrive at her conclusions very quickly
and would deal efficiently with any problem that was handed to
her.

When China took over Tibet, the Dalai Lama fled whilst the
Panchen Lama remained in Tibet under Chinese rule; it was
Indira who advised her father, when the Dalai Lama asked for
asylum, that he should be granted it. This, of course, opened the
door to the Tibetan refugees who came with him across the
mountains. Pandit Nehru, although not quite sure that this was a
wise thing to do, in view of his friendly relations with China,
arranged for the Dalai Lama and his *entourage* to live in the
mountain resort of Mussoorie, where he still is. This friendly attitude towards the Dalai Lama precipitated the hardening of
China's attitude on India's dilatory tactics regarding the Sino-
Indian border issue.

In 1959, when Indira was offered the presidency of the All
India Congress Party, she hesitated briefly before accepting. If
she asked her father, he would say: 'You are old enough to
decide for yourself.' She remembered that when her father had
first been nominated President of the Indian National Congress,
he had been a year younger than she was now. Her acceptance
followed. The position was similar to that of the chairman of any
political party in Britain.

Indian journalists who remember the days of Pandit Nehru's
premiership say that he was a great manipulator but a clever
manipulator. According to these people his daughter has also
inherited this quality, the difference being that her activities can
be traced to her, which was not always possible in the case of her
father.

When Pandit Nehru had wanted to involve his daughter in the
political life of the country, he had prevailed upon Radhakrish-
nan, Chairman of UNESCO, to let Indira work for UNESCO.
This sort of vague cultural career did not interest Indira, so she
did not last long there. Her father's next move was to get her
elected to the Congress Working Committee through U. N.

Dhebar, the President of the Congress Party, in 1954/55; it was the first step, it is said, to Indira's election as President of the Congress Party in 1959. Was this also manipulated by Jawaharlal Nehru? This has been suggested, but then the present Prime Minister of India has many enemies who have been proved to be false prophets regarding her capabilities and political acumen.

Inder Gujral, India's Minister of Information and Broadcasting, relates how he and his brother were having breakfast with Pandit Nehru when the news came of Indira's election as Congress Party President. According to Gujral, Pandit Nehru's surprise and his general reaction could not have been more genuine. He said : 'I hope her health will permit her to carry out her arduous duties.' Others say that he always intended this to be her training for the job of Prime Minister, which he had in mind for her, as his successor.

One of the first things Indira Gandhi did as Congress President, was to try to recruit younger people onto the Congress Committees. She made out a retiring list of people who were too old to be active in Party work. On this list she also included her father, but of course as Prime Minister he remained the leader of the Party. The vacancies she filled with younger men and women. Pandit Nehru was proud of her energy, affection and integrity – qualities which she had inherited from her mother. When he attended a Congress Party meeting under her Presidency, he saluted her and said : 'At first Indira was my friend and adviser, then she became my companion and now she is my chief.' From her father it was indeed a great compliment.

The Congress Party in Kerala (S. India) was weak and the State had a communist government which had tried to govern according to its ideology. This was, of course, not to the liking of the Catholic Church and other vested interests. The Catholic Church was powerful and ran a large number of fee-paying schools. Kerala has the highest figure for literacy in India. One of the Church's quarrels with the communist government was that it was about to make education free and open more state schools. Others had complaints about taxes, victimization and dispossession. No sooner was Indira Gandhi elected than all these complaints were placed before her by the Congress Party, with allegations of a breakdown of law and order. She therefore asked her father to make use of the President's special powers to unseat the communist government in Kerala and temporarily install President's rule until the climate was right for an election. Pandit Nehru disagreed and said that it would be wrong to unseat a democratically elected government; for him this was not democracy. His daughter argued that this government was not working for democracy, but trying to bring in communism; should not one therefore prevent it in order to defend democracy? Seeing that her father was not willing to take such a step, Indira told him that if the Prime Minister of India was not willing to unseat the communist government, she would rally all the women in protest against the Kerala Government. Her counsel prevailed and the first President's rule was instituted in Kerala. President's rule meant the autocratic rule of a Governor, appointed by the Central Government, with advisers.

In Orissa, on the eastern seaboard, Indira found the Congress Party bankrupt of influence and two new parties formed, which were gaining influence. She flew to the State capital and advised the Congress Government there that if it was to avoid being pushed out of power, it must form a coalition government with the Ganatantra Parished, a new party including among its members both the hereditary princes and their subjects. With the Congress Party candidate as Chief Minister, a coalition government was formed in Orissa. It had been a situation which, but for Indira Gandhi's intervention and tactics, could have led to the routing of the Congress Party.

Indira Gandhi, during her Presidency, showed tremendous energy, an energy that the old-fashioned Party machine was incapable of matching. All the same, her period in office gave her a good idea of what was wrong with the Party and why it was losing prestige in so many States. She did what she could to remedy the immediate situation. In 1960, she went to Kerala and as a result of her skilful tactics, the Congress Party won with the help of the other anti-communist parties, although its majority was small. The Congress alliance with the Muslim League brought unfavourable reactions. Indira Gandhi's argument was that the practicalities of the situation demanded this alliance. Her approach, she said, had been pragmatic.

A further demonstration of Indira's determination and ability involved the recurring clashes between Gujarati-speaking and Maharathi-speaking peoples in the State of Bombay in 1959-60. The Maharashtrians wanted their own State with its own economy, and its own language. Morarji Desai, a Gujerati, was the Chief Minister – the same man who was later to create so many problems for Indira. The Maharashtrians felt that all the economic prizes and top posts were going to the Gujaratis, and that only inferior positions fell to them. The two groups did not speak or understand each other's languages.

Pandit Nehru, who had once, with shrewd insight, written to his daughter from prison : 'A politician wants to have a say on every subject and he always pretends to know much more than he actually does. He has to be watched carefully;' failed to apply it when a practical case demanded that he practise what he had preached. He considered Morarji Desai a strong Chief Minister and able to solve the dispute. He was quite unaware of the strong-arm tactics being used in Bombay by the Gujarati Chief Minister, but Indira was aware of it and she pressed her father to end the riots by dividing the large province into two units – Gujarat and Maharashtra. When the division was made, the city of Bombay, for the control of which both sides had fought, fell to Maharashtra. The city was and still is India's greatest commercial city, with most commerce controlled by Gujaratis and Sindhi refugees from Pakistan. A situation was thus created whereby although most big business was in the hands of Gujaratis, the bulk of the population was Maharashtrian. This has remained a sore point with the Gujaratis. Pandit Nehru felt he owed something to Morarji Desai for this partitioning of Bombay State, and he was given a seat in the Central Cabinet in New Delhi.

After more than a decade of communal harmony, rioting

suddenly broke out in the small country town of Jabalpur in Madhya Pradesh. Of all the Congress leaders, it was Indira who flew to the disturbed area, where Hindu fanatics had created a terrifying atmosphere for the Muslim minority, who were living from day to day in fear of mob violence. When other people arrived in Jabalpur to see what could be done to help, they found that Indira had already been there; she had reassured the panic-stricken Muslims, reprimanded the police and told them not to fail again in their duty, and had returned to report to her father. Pandit Nehru was greatly distressed to hear of this fresh outbreak of religious strife after so many peaceful years. Were his ideas of a secular state any more than a utopian dream? Indira reassured him with his own assertion that strength and fearlessness would keep India a secular state.

In between her duties as hostess and her visits to foreign countries, Indira also remembered the villagers of Phulpur, near Allahabad in Uttar Pradesh, who had elected Jawaharlal Nehru to Lok-Sabha. She found time to visit them and to assure them of her father's and her own thoughts for them and their welfare. She found out their needs and said she would do what she could for them.

After one year in office as Congress Party President, Indira Gandhi refused to stand for re-election. She was worried about her father and felt that it was necessary for her to be more at home. Her first political appointment had brought her a great deal of experience and she had got to know the people at grass roots level. Many people did not consider that she had proved herself a competent and diplomatic President. Some condemned her actions in Kerala. Others said that she had taken the hint, that the Party had rejected her and that she had not come up to its expectations.

Indira's term of office had also given her enormous insight into the monolithic, cumbersome, resolution-passing Party machine. This was to be of great use to her in later years. She knew that for the Congress Party to regain its power and prestige without the magic of Jawaharlal Nehru, there must be a great deal of rethinking and readjustment. Resolutions had to be wrested from the Minutes of the meetings and made concrete. Her father was getting old and his responsibilities to the country as Prime Minister were enormous and all consuming. If the Party was to continue as the Party of Gandhi and Nehru, somebody had to take that responsibility and be prepared to work away from the limelight. Indira could not believe that among the large membership of the Congress Party nobody could be found. Her principle duty at that moment in time, however, was to care for her father. She had given up her private life for this purpose and now he needed her more than ever.

5

End of an Epoch

The death of Jawaharlal Nehru marked the end of an epoch, for the country he had loved and served, and also for his daughter. She felt she had arrived at a point when everything familiar and secure lay behind her, while her future was uncertain. She recognized the security which, even during her lonely childhood, had been symbolized by her father. His letters, his companionship, his love and understanding had been like a protective covering. His loss overwhelmed her and drained her of outward emotion.

As he lay in state he was as impersonal as the Taj Mahal – he belonged to the nation, she was only one individual among 400 million. Twenty-four hours earlier her position in his life had been special : it was Indira who had been responsible for her father's well-being and their closeness had been very real. Death had dropped the final curtain on all that had been, and had given him, however briefly, to the people whom he had loved for their last homage.

Indira was frozen in grief. She stood like a carved image, barefoot, for hours it seemed to lookers-on, by his bier while he lay in state for the millions who loved him to take their last look at the well-known face. Always aloof and withdrawn by nature, her father's death appeared to have taken away whatever life there had been in her. The blood had drained away from her face into tears which froze around her heart. She could not shed them.

The young man of twenty-five who had been the inspiration and idol of young India, not only in his own generation, but in

66

the one that followed, through all the tedious and harrowing years of the fight for independence, had become in the last five years of his life something of a liability for his colleagues in government, although still the well-beloved of the people. Nehru had ruled India as absolutely as any monarch from 1947 to 1964, but his ideas were democratic, his ideals socialist. From 1947 onwards, his main objective was to build a socialist state in India. His determination was unwavering, his theories correct, but his knowledge of economics was incomplete and he overruled his advisers if they did not agree with him.

Jawaharlal Nehru *was* India, there was no doubt of that. His intellect was sharp and his ability to work immense. After the death of Sardar Vallabhai Patel, he was a Gulliver among Lilliputians, who resented this and only bided their time. During his rule, his colleagues rubber-stamped his decisions, although most of them disapproved of his policies. If they did not like what he wanted to do, they just had to accept it. Nehru was not afraid that his leadership would ever be challenged – there was no 'second line' which could aspire to dethrone him. He had never built up any potential successors, not through fear, but because he did not think it necessary.

As Nehru grew older and frailer in health, his opinions became more dogmatic and he defended them with all the obstinacy and wilfulness which had characterized him from youth. Only now his associates found it intolerable and were not prepared to bow down to the master. They had discovered that he was not infallible, but as yet they lacked the courage to defy him, to try and wrest power from him, for the weight of the people's will was wholly with him. He was the only person they trusted. There grew the inevitable rumours that in a bid for power, his colleagues were plotting to get rid of him by working on his frail health, because they knew that death was the only thing that could end the power and glory which Nehru still enjoyed. Nobody foresaw the vacuum his death would leave, because power-hungry politicians were each and every one anxious to occupy his place. Through the difficult and troublesome days, as Indira saw her father age, she guarded him and helped him as only she could. If possible they grew closer to each other; if possible he depended more and more on her, refusing to change his way of life – at least outwardly, although the inevitable physical weaknesses of age were slowly creeping up on him. But the clarity of his mind was unaffected, as were the visions of a self-sufficient, prosperous India on the road to socialism, which had been his objective since youth.

In 1962, Jawaharlal Nehru suffered an attack of ill-health which was at first thought to be influenza. It began after a normal day's work, which started for him at 6.30 a.m. and ended at 7.30 p.m., sometimes later. He had not been feeling too well in the morning, but had dismissed it as a minor ailment. Indira was away on a lecture tour of the USA and Krishna, Nehru's younger sister, was filling in for her. Very soon it became clear that Nehru was seriously ill and for two weeks he ran a high temperature and grew weaker day by day. His sister was frantic with anxiety, since whatever the doctors gave to him appeared either to have no effect, or to make him worse. Krishna felt desperately alone with all the hatchet-faced men of Nehru's Cabinet round her, waiting for him to die. She was also overcome with a sense of her responsibility to Indira and cabled her to come back. The doctors, on the other hand, were sending Indira reassuring cables, telling her not to give up her lecture tour.

Finally, Krishna decided to telephone the Nehru family physician, Dr B. C. Roy, who lived in Calcutta and was also the Chief Minister of the State of West Bengal. But every time she tried, she was told that all telephone lines to Calcutta were engaged or down. Later she found that her telegrams to Calcutta were never sent. In desperation, she appealed to a quiet little man, who was later to play a very important part in the history of India, Lal Bahadur Shastri, the Minister for Railways, to get a telephone line for her to Dr Roy, which he did. Jawaharlal Nehru's condition grew worse, but neither the medical men nor his Cabinet showed much anxiety. The arrival of Dr Roy who, at the age of eighty-four, exuded health and confidence, brought a feeling of relief not only to the patient but also to his sister. Dr Roy scrapped the treatment that had so far been prescribed, supervised Nehru's treatment and medicines for three days and, when he left for Calcutta, saw his patient on the way to recovery. Nehru's sister and his close and loyal associates saw something sinister in the way Nehru had been gradually drained of his powers of resistance to fight his illness.

A factor which contributed to the decline of Nehru's spirits at this time was the state of India's relations with China over the question of the North-East Frontier. Friendly talks between India and China had been in progress since 1950. Nehru's deep sympathy for China was longstanding, dating from the 'thirties when Japan invaded China and occupied Manchuria. He visited Peking soon after the People's Republic had been established and genuinely believed in the possibility of peaceful co-existence and that India and China together would bring a new age to Asia. When Chou En-lai visited India in 1954, a treaty of friendship was signed embodying five principles for continuing friendship. Indians and Chinese are brothers, it was declared. Nehru genuinely believed in the good faith of the Chinese.

The Chinese, however, felt that there was one outstanding matter which ought to be clarified. This was the question of the MacMahon line, which formed an arbitrary border between China and India across the lower ranges of the Himalayas. Since India had not maintained any of the other British-determined boundaries, the Chinese felt that there should be no difficulty in reaching an amicable settlement. Nehru was no less agreeable to discussion, but his colleagues saw in this approach land hunger on the part of the Chinese. They forced Nehru to prolong the discussions, hoping, some felt, that if Nehru died or was displaced, friendship with China need not continue. These men were all anxious for Nehru to forget the Chinese and pursue friendship with the United States. Krishna Menon, the Defence Minister, was the only one who continued to advise Nehru to make a deal with China. Indira also advised her father to come to an understanding on the question; she felt that China's patience was nearly exhausted. The discussions had been carried on for more than ten years and since China was not a dictatorship, Chou En-lai must show results to his people. But Nehru's Cabinet colleagues would not agree to giving up any land, however useless and arbitrarily apportioned to India.

Nehru would have overruled his colleagues if he had suspected that China's mood was aggressive, but he did not believe this to be the case. His friendship for China was genuine, but his political sagacity did not tell him that friendships can be overstrained, especially international ones. When in the autumn of 1962 China crossed the Se-La Pass in the Himalayas, 8,000 feet high and thought to be impregnable, China dealt a serious blow at Nehru. He had, perhaps naively, believed in the five principles of friendship and he could not understand why China should want to invade India or claim any Indian territory. As for the Chinese, they felt that this area of the mountains was part of China and, after having inflicted heavy casualties on Indian troops, withdrew to a line which they considered should be the real boundary. But the first casualty of that short war was India's Prime Minister. It preyed on him as a betrayal of friendship and his Cabinet colleagues were not slow in making the wound deeper. For the first time mistrust of his own judgement crept into Nehru's mind. He brooded.

Early in 1964, while attending a meeting of the Congress Party in the capital of the State of Orissa on the north-eastern shores of the Bay of Bengal, Nehru had a stroke. Indira was with him, doctors were flown out to attend to him, but it was some time before he could be moved to New Delhi. With Indira at his side, he slowly returned almost to his old self, except that he now dragged one foot. Very sadly, it became apparent to his daughter that her father, who even when he attained his seventieth birthday had been able to run up the stairs of the Prime Minister's residence, would never do so again. It was difficult for her to accept that he would have to slow down. He still made speeches standing up, he carried on his full duties as Prime Minister, but there were many who said that he could no longer take swift decisions, and that his digressions at Committees left the members ignorant of what he wanted to say. The keeness of his intellect, people said, had also been blunted after his last illness, but for five months he lived a fairly normal life.

Early on 27 May, Nehru awoke in great pain. Indira hurried to his bedside and within a quarter of an hour the doctor arrived. He had obviously been suffering for some time, as the aorta had burst. Blood transfusion was immediately necessary, but he had a rare blood group. Only Indira's blood was similar, and readily available, but she gave it, glad to be able to do something. It was suggested that an operation might save him; she agreed, but medical opinion was conflicting, and the Cabinet did not wish to take any risks. So the Prime Minister was not moved to hospital for the operation. He died in his home later that afternoon.

For Indira a world ended. If she sobbed in the privacy of her room, to the world she showed the face of grief carved out of stone. Her loss was too great, too immediate and too much with her. If grief shared is truly lessened, then the genuine sorrow of the millions of the people of India, far and near, should have helped her. Even children mourned him. He had been their friend. Tributes poured in from all over the world and Prime Ministers and heads of state arrived to be present for the funeral of a man they had held in the greatest esteem.

Jawaharlal Nehru's Will was brief. He had nothing to leave. His private earnings had been the royalties from his books and his modest salary as Prime Minister. He had been an agnostic and had abhorred all the outward pomp and ceremony of organized religion. But in death it was impossible for him to avoid it, although his Will contained clear instructions for the simplest of cremations.

He had written :

I wish to declare in all earnestness that I do not want any religious ceremonies performed for me after my death. I do not believe in any such ceremonies and to submit to them, even as a matter of form, would be hypocrisy.

I have received so much love and affection from the Indian people that nothing I can do can repay even a small fraction of it and indeed there can be no repayment of so precious a thing as affection. . . .

When I die, I should like my body to be cremated. If I die in a foreign country, my body should be cremated and sent to Allahabad. A small handful of these ashes should be thrown into the Ganga and the major portion of them disposed of in the manner indicated below. No part of these ashes should be retained or preserved.

My desire to have a handful of my ashes thrown into the Ganga at Allahabad has no religious significance; so far as I am concerned, I have no religious sentiment in the matter. I have been attached to the Ganga and the Jumna rivers at Allahabad, ever since my childhood and as I have grown older the attachment has grown. I have watched their varying moods as the seasons changed and have often thought of the history and myth and tradition and song and story that have become attached to them through the long ages and become part of their flowing waters.

The Ganga, especially, is the River of India, beloved of her people, round which are entwined her racial memories, her hopes and fears, her songs of triumph, her victories and defeats. She has been a symbol of India's age-long culture and civilization, ever changing, ever flowing and yet ever the same Ganga. She reminds me of the snow-covered peaks and valleys of the Himalayas, which I have loved so much, and of the rich and vast plains below, where my life and work have been cast. Smiling and dancing in the morning sunlight and dark and flowing and full of mystery as the evening shadows fall; a narrow, slow and graceful stream in winter and a vast and swirling torrent during the monsoon, broad-bosomed, almost as the sea, and with something of the sea's power to destroy, the Ganga has been to me a symbol of the past of India running into the present and flowing on to the great ocean of the future. And though I have discarded much of past tradition and custom and am anxious that India rid herself of all shackles that bind and constrain her and divide her people and suppress vast numbers of them and prevent the free development of the body and the spirit, though I seek all this, yet I do not wish to cut myself from the past completely. I am proud of that great inheritance that has been and is ours and I am conscious that I too, like all of us, am a link in an unbroken chain which goes back to the dawn of history in the immemorial past of India. That chain I would not break for I treasure it and seek inspiration from it. And as witness of this desire of mine and as my last homage to India's cultural inheritance, I am making this request that a handful of my ashes be thrown into the Ganga at Allahabad to be carried to the great ocean that washes India's shores.

The major portion of my ashes should, however, be disposed of otherwise. I want these to be carried high up in the air in an aeroplane and scattered from that height over the fields where the peasants of India toil, so that they might become an indistinguishable part of India.

Jawaharlal Nehru.

Indira requested Lal Bahadur Shastri, for whom she and her father had the greatest regard, to arrange the implementation of her father's last wishes.

However, the religious atmosphere could not be kept out – after all, the citizens of India also had their ideas for a final tribute. Religion is a way of life for millions of Indians. The first approach, however, was made by an Indian Catholic priest with about a dozen small boys from his orphanage. He told Indira : 'We will be very unobtrusive if you will let the boys sing "Ave Maria" for your father – a hymn he loved and he loved children. They will not make a noise.' Nobody had the heart to refuse. After that a Hindu priest was chanting his mantras in one corner *sotto voce*; on the other side a *maulvi* (Muslim priest) called quietly upon *allah*. Thus the unity of India, which Nehru believed in and upheld, was symbolized at his death.

The funeral was a slow-moving affair as the cortège moved through the streets of New Delhi and Old Delhi. Jawaharlal Nehru's body was borne on a gun carriage covered with the

national flag. Indira and her younger son Sanjoy followed the
bier. Rajiv, her eldest, was at Cambridge and would not be back
in India until the following day. The temperature was in the
hundreds Fahrenheit. In India funerals wait for nobody – climate
and custom make the rule. The cremation was to be by the river
Jumna, close to where Gandhi had been cremated. There were
great crowds along the road, wailing and bemoaning as his
daughter could not.

A funeral pyre of sandalwood had been made ready, anointed
with *ghee* (melted butter). Jawaharlal Nehru's body was laid on
it, piled with more sandalwood and flowers. Sanjoy, his grandson,
as his closest male relative present, had the terrifying task of
plunging a flaming torch into the pyre to light it. A formidable
duty for a fourteen year old boy. Indira took her final farewell of
the one single person whose influence had been paramount in her
life, whose love had cherished and protected her until now. Who
could measure her sorrow? It had temporarily taken away from
her the power to act. She had known that this would happen, but
when it had actually happened, it had found her unprepared.

Much still had to be done that was painful. Accompanied by
her aunts and of course her two sons, Indira made the long and
dusty journey to Allahabad, carrying her father's ashes in an urn.
The journey was not only uncomfortable but slow, because the
train was halted at every station to enable people to pay their last
homage to the man who had for so many years guided their lives.
The nearer they got to Allahabad, the thicker the crowds became.
Finally, after twenty-five hours, a journey which normally does
not take more than fourteen, Indira and her *entourage* reached
Anand Bhawan – once the abode of joy and happiness. Today
there was only sorrow and remembrance. There were also the
relatives and people of Allahabad to meet, a painful prolongation
of the events in New Delhi.

Indira had brought with her also a tiny box, containing the
ashes of her mother. She explained to her aunts that her father
had kept them on the table beside his bed. He wanted them to be
immersed with his own ashes in the Ganga. The following morn-

ing Indira, accompanied by her sons and her two aunts, was rowed to the confluence of the Ganga and the Jumna, for all Hindus a place of great sanctity. There her father's final wishes were fulfilled.

Until and even after her return to New Delhi Indira had been totally unconcerned with the fate of the Government and its construction. Like her father, she felt sure that somebody competent would be found. She was totally overcome with her own loss and filled with a determination that there should be a fitting memorial to her father. To this she would now devote herself. Nothing was further from her thoughts than the affairs of state.

Lal Bahadur Shastri had been chosen as Prime Minister. He was a man of great integrity, strength of character and intelligence. He was acceptable to the people since he had enjoyed Nehru's confidence and therefore they trusted him more than any other member of the old Cabinet. It was, however, felt in Government circles that if Nehru's daughter could be associated in some ministerial capacity, it would create even greater confidence.

On Indira's return from Allahabad, Lal Bahadur Shastri went to see her. She asked him to arrange for the disposal of the rest of her father's ashes as he had directed. The new Prime Minister told her that he did not wish to take up residence in the house which had for so long been her father's since India had become independent. He felt that the erstwhile Prime Minister's house should become the nucleus of a Jawaharlal Nehru Memorial. Indira was delighted with this idea. Then Lal Bahadur spoke of his real mission, to ask Indira to join his Cabinet as Minister for External Affairs. He explained to her that he was a man who had never left India, except to go to Nepal once. She had been all over the world; she had known many world personalities, travelling with her father and acting as his hostess in New Delhi. She would be of the greatest help to him.

For the first time since her father's death, Indira broke down and wept and begged Lal Bahadur Shastri to spare her, to give her some time to realize her loss. She was not able to take in anything at present, least of all a position of such importance. 'I should like to have six months of quietness before I take up any position in Government,' she said. She would like to devote herself to building a memorial to her father. She could not take on such tremendous responsibilities as he proposed for her, her mind would not be able to compass these duties fully. On that occasion Lal Bahadur could say no more. Her grief was too intense.

Lal Bahadur Shastri was, however, a determined man and he returned again and again, saying that Jawaharlal's daughter would bring prestige to his Cabinet. If Indira did not want to take on the External Affairs Ministry, would she not accept the Information portfolio? This would accustom her to being in office without entailing arduous duties. She could still carry on with the plans for her father's memorial. Lal Bahadur's importunity finally broke down her resistance. Indira agreed to take the Information portfolio, but she requested that the taking of the oath ceremony be postponed for a while. Shortly afterwards, she was sworn in by the President as Minister for Information and Broadcasting.

Indira's next step was to move out of the mansion she had occupied with her father. The Government allotted her a house at 1, Safderjung Road, which has now become famous as the Prime Minister's residence. It was a house of moderate size and part of it had to be used as her office. It had a small garden, too small for the number of people who still came in the early morning as they used to do to see her father. She talked to them, for it was one way of keeping in touch with the people. They spoke of their problems and, if she could, Indira would place them before the right people, who could perhaps solve them. She liked talking to the people who sought her out. They were a source of courage and inspiration. Their loyalty towards her and their genuine love and affection for her date from that time.

As part of her work in her position as Information Minister, Indira injected new life into broadcasting in India which, until then, had not realized its full potential. The possibilities of developing radio and television to entertain and instruct the illiterate masses were tremendous. She introduced material concerned with social problems, such as family planning, into the radio programmes. Until then, All India Radio had been a mouthpiece for the Government alone. She opened the doors to the Opposition, and to other controversial points of view. She also introduced new and unorthodox people onto the Board of Film Censors, hoping to liberalize its traditional point of view.

Frank Moraes recalls that at this period he suggested to Indira that she should develop also the television service, which could even more effectively reach out to the people. She had been disturbed by the bad press the Government and the Congress Party had been suffering, and Moraes suggested that television could help to balance this publicity. Indira Gandhi agreed that it was a good idea, but asked how such a programme could be financed. Moraes suggested commercial television, and he reports: 'Her reply was strangely girlish, for she said, "My father would not have liked it." But, of course, she is now going ahead with the idea – seven years later.'

Even in her minor role as a Cabinet Minister, she undertook two important visits abroad. She was invited to the Soviet Union by Kosygin, who had succeeded Khruschev as Premier and who reaffirmed the continuation of Soviet economic and arms aid to India. The policy formulated during her father's lifetime would continue. Indira also went to America for the opening of the Jawaharlal Memorial Exhibition in New York by Vice President Hubert Humphrey. This exhibition was later to tour world capitals. It told in words and pictures the story of the life and times of Jawaharlal Nehru.

When the Commonwealth Prime Ministers' Conference was held in London in 1965, Prime Minister Shastri did not attend it. He suggested that Indira should go on his behalf, feeling that her experience of many such conferences with her father qualified her uniquely for the task. This set in motion a great deal of rivalry and it was urged that the delegation should go under the joint leadership of T. T. Krishnamachari who was back in the Cabinet and Indira Gandhi. Indira resented this. She did go to London, but attended no social functions jointly. It was Indira's first visit to England since her father's death and a great many old friends were naturally anxious to meet her and convey their condolences personally. Indira tried to see all those who wished to see her. She was in every way as she had been, reserved, unassuming, but her sorrow was stamped on her face. Her loss was too great to conceal from anybody.

At home, Mrs Gandhi's interest in social welfare continued alongside her interest in the development of broadcasting for the people of India. She encouraged the manufacture of cheap transistor radio sets, capable of receiving at least three Indian stations. During her time as Minister, she was able to double broadcasting hours. Indira would tour the villages to ascertain the possibilities for bringing radio and television to the people. She was criticized for not being in her office at all times, but did not allow this to trouble her, since she was doing her job as she thought best.

At the time a controversy was raging about Hindi, which had been nominated as the official language of India in the Constitution. Not a word of Hindi was spoken along the eastern seaboard of India. In 1963-64 the situation was particularly bad in the State of Madras and other Tamil-speaking areas. Twenty years was the period allotted under the Constitution for Hindi to be established as the State language. The twentieth year was fast approaching and non-Hindi speaking people were becoming greatly alarmed. Indira went to Madras and spoke to angry crowds; she assured them that she would find out if there was an alternative solution. On the basis of her advice and her report, Lal Bahadur Shastri was able to secure a revision of the Constitution so that English could 'temporarily' be retained as the 'associate' official language. A 'language war' was thus averted.

Even then nobody could have forecast the next stage in the career of Indira Gandhi. Shastri had proved a strong Prime Minister and parliamentary affairs were going on as well as before. However, the economic scene was full of problems and hazards and the Third Five Year Plan had been temporarily suspended.

Some people had looked upon Indira's ministerial appointment as a handout, received because she was her father's daughter. They did not resent it, but neither did they feel that there was any great merit in her to enable her to go further. She attracted little attention, neither did she seek it. The ordinary people of India were happy that she was in the Government and that she still held the 'open house' early morning meetings, as her father used to do. All those who came to see her placed their problems before her in full confidence that she would try to do whatever was possible on their behalf.

6

Apprenticeship

The death of Lal Bahadur Shastri, India's second Prime Minister since independence, flung the country into despair. He had been a good man and a competent administrator. He had successfully steered the country through the India-Pakistan War of 1965. He died, after a short rule of two and a half years, at Tashkent in the USSR. The previous night he and Ayub Khan, the President of Pakistan, with the help of Alexei Kosygin, the Soviet Prime Minister, had signed a peace treaty which would bring stability to the sub-continent.

New Delhi became a very busy place when it was known that Shastri had died. The noise of grinding axes rose in a crescendo. Anybody who had the slightest chance of succeeding Shastri arrived on the scene to present themselves before the Congress Party President, Kamraj Nadar – 'the kingmaker'. Most of them were non-starters, but four possibles finally emerged, though none of these could be considered really eligible candidates.

Mrs Vijayalakshmi Pandit resigned her governorship of Bombay State, flew back from her lecture tour of the USA and came to New Delhi. She hoped, on the basis of her background and family, to make an impact on the Congress Party Chief. She had all the Nehru charm and vitality. Mrs Pandit had been Ambassador to Moscow and Washington. She had indifferent records in both capitals, but she had been most successful in her two periods as High Commissioner in London. She had also achieved some stature as President of the United Nations General Assembly.

Gulzarilal Nanda, twice acting Prime Minister on the death of two Prime Ministers, felt that if he was good enough to fill the gap temporarily, he was good enough for the post. He was well-known within the Congress Party as an orthodox and bigoted Hindu. He too became a prospective candidate.

Morarji Desai, who until lately had been Finance Minister, was well-known for his puritanical outlook. He had framed the prohibition laws and believed in rigid moral discipline. He had been in the Government for many years, and had been Deputy Prime Minister in the Nehru Government. His claim to the position of Prime Minister was obvious: he was a Gandhian. He had a large following among those who resented the Nehru way of socialism – the princes, the landlords, the bankers, the merchant princes and the commercial houses, and was considered to stand a good chance of winning the post.

Y. B. Chavan, from Maharashtra, the Defence Minister, having brought the Pakistan War to a successful close, counted on the loyalty of the army. Chavan was a strong man and might be a competent administrator. But his neighbours feared that he would favour his own State at their expense.

Kamraj kept court like some dark, fat, benign god of joy and prosperity, but with a shrewd brain behind his calm exterior. Within the Party his word was paramount.

Indira Gandhi had taken no part in this competition. She was an interested but aloof onlooker. She had not the slightest idea that this was, in reality, her own moment of destiny.

Kamraj Nadar's main preoccupation was how to get the Congress Party back into power in the General Elections of 1967 at which the communists were certain to present a real threat. He even toyed with the idea of making a bid for the Prime Minister-ship himself, but he knew that internationally he was unqualified – he could speak only Tamil and no foreign language, not even English. Being a realist, he dismissed the four possible candidates one by one: Morarji Desai, with his narrow-minded puritanism and sectarianism, would not be able to carry the whole country; neither would Gulzarilal Nanda, with his Hindu orthodoxy. One

had to bear in mind the 100 million Muslim minority. Y. B.
Chavan as a Maharashtrian was also unacceptable to the neigh-
bouring State of Gujarat. Vijayalakshmi Pandit's only qualification was that she was a Nehru, still a name to conjure with in
India. If that was a qualification, why not Indira Gandhi?
Jawaharlal Nehru's daughter would have tremendous appeal for
the masses and for young people. She was young, she had been
President of the All India National Congress, she was already a
Minister. She was quiet and aloof and did not seem strong enough
to resist Kamraj and the old guard or, as they later came to be
called, the Syndicate; she might even be useful to Kamraj's own
ambitions while he tried to master the English language. Having
reasoned thus, Kamraj announced that, after a great deal of
deliberation, he felt Indira Gandhi was the right person to succeed
Lal Bahadur Shastri as Prime Minister.

Kamraj told Indira of his decision and that it was her duty to
take on the job. Nobody was more surprised than Indira herself.
All the other contestants withdrew, with the exception of Morarji
Desai, on the extreme Right. He was prepared to take it to a
ballot of the Congress Parliamentary Party, so sure was he of his
following. While Nehru was alive he had schemed for power
without success; after Nehru's death the comparatively unknown
Lal Bahadur Shastri had been chosen and now the prize was
again slipping through his fingers into the hands of this young,
inexperienced girl. Morarji Desai would fight it out with her.

Nanda and Chavan withdrew because they did not wish to
cross swords with Kamraj. In the long run it would not pay to
fall foul of the Congress Party Chief. They did not for a moment
imagine that Morarji Desai could lose. In fact they were already
wondering what they could get out of his victory.

Kamraj was sure that his nominee would win. He called
together the Chief Ministers of the ten States in which there were
Congress majorities to tell them of his choice of candidate, and
also instructed them that their State representatives in the Lok-
Sabha Parliamentary Party should vote for Indira Gandhi.

16 January, 1966 was the day fixed for the ballot. If Indira

was nervous, she certainly preserved her usual calm exterior. She herself, one imagines, was by no means sure of her victory. Tension mounted all over India. In Delhi it was at its height. There was a great deal of lobbying and canvassing, in which Indira did not participate.

Early that morning, before she went to the Lok-Sabha, Indira carried out three 'pilgrimages'. First she went to say a prayer at the Gandhi Shrine at *Rajghat*, on the banks of the river Jumna, where he had been cremated. Then she went to *Santi Vana* – the Abode of Peace – also on the shores of the Jumna, to her father's memorial, where his body had been committed to the flames. She paid her tribute of remembrance and gratitude to the two persons who had the greatest influence on her life and had made it possible for her to arrive at the position in which she stood that day, and to fulfil the career she had to carve out for herself. Finally, she visited the house which had been her home with Pandit Nehru, and went into her father's room, which still stood exactly as it had been on the day he died. On a writing pad lying by his bedside she saw three lines of a poem by Robert Frost, which Nehru had scribbled on it. He had loved those lines:

> The woods are lovely, dark and deep,
> But I have promises to keep,
> And miles to go before I sleep.

The words were very significant for Indira.

On that day, Indira also remembered the advice in one of her father's letters to her from prison, which he had often repeated to her: 'Be brave and all the rest follows. If you are brave you will not fear and will not do anything of which you are ashamed.'

With such thoughts in her mind, her head held high, austerely dressed in white handspun cotton with a shawl draped round her, she entered the central hall of Lok-Sabha, where the Congress Parliamentary Party was assembled for the ballot. The only other contestant, her rival Morarji Desai, was already seated in the front benches, unsmiling and dour. Indira passed him and took a seat in the rear of the hall. Her only outward concession to the occasion was a red rose pinned to her shawl in memory of her father, who used always to wear one pinned to his waistcoat or jacket.

Outside Lok-Sabha the crowds grew thicker, with reporters and newsmen poised for the announcement. The clamour of voices increased as speculation about the result of the ballot circled the building. No news, however, came from within to give any idea of how the voting was going.

It was 3 p.m. when the counting was finished and Kamraj announced the results in Tamil. The smile on his face increased the frown on Morarji Desai's, for the result was clear. Then it was translated into English : Indira Gandhi had obtained 355 votes to Morarji Desai's 169. There was jubilation among her followers. Kamraj asked her to come to the dais and address the Members. Newsmen rushed in, cameras flashed and television lights were focused on her. A crowd of more than ten thousand went delirious with joy when she reappeared outside, elected their Prime Minister. Exhausted, bewildered and happy, she went home to find her house invaded by many of the ordinary people of India who, in their excitement, wanted to catch a glimpse of her. Cordons of police had to be called in to protect her from the affection of the onrushing crowds.

On 25 January, 1966, Indira took her oath of office before the President of India. On 26 January, Republic Day, she made her first broadcast to the people as Prime Minister of India. These are some of the things she said :

My own approach to the vast problems which confront us is one of humility. However, the tradition left by Gandhi and my father, and my own unbounded faith in the people of India give me strength and confidence. Time and again India has given evidence of an indomitable spirit.

In recent years, as in the past, she has shown unmistakable courage and capacity for meeting new challenges. There is a firm base of Indianness which will withstand any trial.

The coming months bristle with difficulties. We have

innumerable problems requiring urgent action. The rains have failed us, causing drought in many parts. As a result, agricultural production, which is still precariously dependent on weather and rainfall, has suffered a sharp decline. Economic aid from abroad and earnings from export, have not come to us in the measure expected. The lack of foreign exchange has hurt industrial production. Let us not be dismayed or discouraged by these unforeseen difficulties. Let us face them boldly. Let us learn from our mistakes and resolve not to let them recur. I hope to talk to you from time to time to explain the measures we take and to seek your support for them.

Above all else, we must ensure food to our people in this year of scarcity. This is the first duty of the Government.

We shall give urgent attention to the management and equitable distribution of food grains, both imported and procured at home.

We shall try especially to meet the nutritional needs of mothers and children in the scarcity-affected areas to prevent permanent damage to their health. We cannot afford to take risks where basic food is concerned. We propose, therefore, to import large enough quantities of food grains to bridge this gap. We are grateful to the United States for her sympathetic understanding and prompt help.

Only greater production will solve our food problem. We have now a well thought-out plan to obtain water, chemical fertilizers and new high-yielding varieties of seed, as well as technical advice and credit to farmers.

Our strategy of economic advance assigns a prominent role to the public sector for the rapid expansion of basic industries, power and transport. In our circumstances, this is not only desirable but necessary. It also imposes an obligation to initiate, to construct and manage public sector enterprises efficiently and to produce sufficient profits for further investments.

In economic development, as in other fields of national activity, there is a disconcerting gap between intention and action. To bridge this gap, we should boldly adopt whatever far-reaching changes in administration may be found necessary. We must introduce new organizational patterns and modern tools and techniques of management and administration. We shall instil into govermental machinery greater efficiency and a sense of urgency and make it more responsive to the needs of the people.

In keeping with our heritage, we have followed a policy of peace and friendship with all nations, yet reserved to ourselves the right to independent opinion.

We seek to maintain the friendliest relations with our neighbours and to resolve any disputes peacefully. The Tashkent Declaration is an expression of these sentiments. We shall implement it fully, in letter and spirit. Peace is our aim, but I am keenly aware of the responsibility of Government to preserve the freedom and territorial integrity of the country. We must therefore be alert and keep a constant vigil, strengthening our defences as necessary. The valour, the determination, the courage and sacrifice of our fighting forces have set a magnificent example. My thoughts today go out to the disabled and the families of those who gave their lives.

Peace we want, because there is another war to fight – the war against poverty, disease and ignorance. We have promises to keep to our people – of work, food, clothing and shelter, health and education. The weaker and underprivileged sections of our people – all those who require special measures of social security, have always been and will remain uppermost in my mind. Youth must have greater opportunity. The young people of India must recognize that they will get from their country tomorrow what they give her today. The nation expects them to aspire and to excel.

No matter what our religion, language or State, we are one nation and one people. Let us be strong, tolerant and disciplined, for tolerance and discipline are the very foundations of democracy.

Today I pledge myself anew to the ideals of the builders of our nation – to democracy and secularism, to planned economic and social advance, to peace and friendship among nations. Citizens of India, let us revive our faith in the future. Let us affirm our ability to shape our destiny. We are comrades in a mighty adventure. Let us be worthy of it and of our great country.

Kamraj had given her a hint, even at the hour of Indira's triumph, that as far as he was concerned she could be only a stop-gap Prime Minister until the right candidate was found. Nothing could have better calculated than such a hint to bring Indira Gandhi's independent spirit to the fore. She was fully aware that her adoption as Prime Minister had been agreed so that she could be used as a front for the coming 1967 election, but she bided her time. She also knew where her strength lay – in the people of India. As the Prime Minister, she was determined to remain in touch with them.

The world reaction was one of amazement. The West could not understand how an Asian country like India had elected a woman prime minister, since it was thought that women in eastern countries occupied an inferior position. *The Economist*, commenting from London, described Mrs Gandhi as India's 'untested leader', but went on to say with great political foresight : 'None of this means that Mrs Gandhi will be the front woman for a collective of queenmakers. Whatever she may owe to them, the Prime Minister of India, once in office, is a dispenser of power and patronage like other prime ministers, if not so untrammelled as some. This one is also a woman of strong will and in her opinion of herself, more akin to her father than to the humble Mr Shastri. . . . In the country at large, she has real political assets. Being her father's daughter is one. Within the Congress leadership, Nehru's name is more for public than private obeisance, but it is still powerful with the Indian masses. She has not made herself obnoxious to any part of the country. . . . She is a genuine secularist like her father, which is essential if the confidence of the country's 50 million Moslems is to be maintained. She is conspicuously not a fanatic for Hindi, which is equally essential if the South Indians are to be reassured that the growth of the intended national language will not make them second class citizens. . . .'

The day after her investiture as Prime Minister, Indira was immediately faced with serious problems, inherited from her predecessor – it was indeed a plateful of scorpions that was placed before her.

Chandni Chowk is the historic and famous bazaar of Delhi. It lies in the centre of the city and was built by the Mogul emperor Shah-jehetu at the same time as the Red Fort. This part of Delhi is known as Old Delhi and contains old family houses and residences that have become little more than overcrowded tenements. There is the great Jumma Masjid – the mosque built by the Moguls, there are temples and also the Gurudwera or the worshipping place of the Sikhs. When Indira was elected Prime Minister, dissension was growing between the Punjab Hindus and the Sikhs over the division of the Punjab, half of which had already been apportioned to Pakistan in 1947. The quarrel was again mainly one of language. The Sikhs had been agitating for their own State since independence but further fragmentation of the already partitioned State of Punjab had not seemed viable to the early Congress rulers and politicians. All that they had been too pre-occupied to do now fell upon the shoulders of Indira Gandhi. The situation was exacerbated by the Punjab politicians who favoured Punjabi Hindus rather than Sikhs. This had led to hunger strikes and demonstrations by the Sikhs.

This was the background to the tense situation in *Chandni Chowk,* where rioting had begun, the Sikhs defending those who had taken shelter in the Gurudwera and the Gurudwera itself, against the threatening, jibing Hindus. The inhabitants of *Chandni Chowk* tried nervously to efface themselves from the scene. Firm action was clearly required, but few people felt that a woman Prime Minister would risk her presence on the spot. However, it was not long before a motor cycle, its siren screeching, roared into the centre, followed by a police car, behind which was another car with its windows up. It stopped at the Gurudwera and people wondered aloud : 'Who is it?' Then someone in the crowd said: 'Don't you recognize your Prime Minister, Indira Gandhi?', as she stepped out of the car. The crowd saw her talking to both factions and they subsequently saw them slink away like shamefaced hooligans.

1 Indira Gandhi as a child, with her parents Jawaharlal and Kamala Nehru

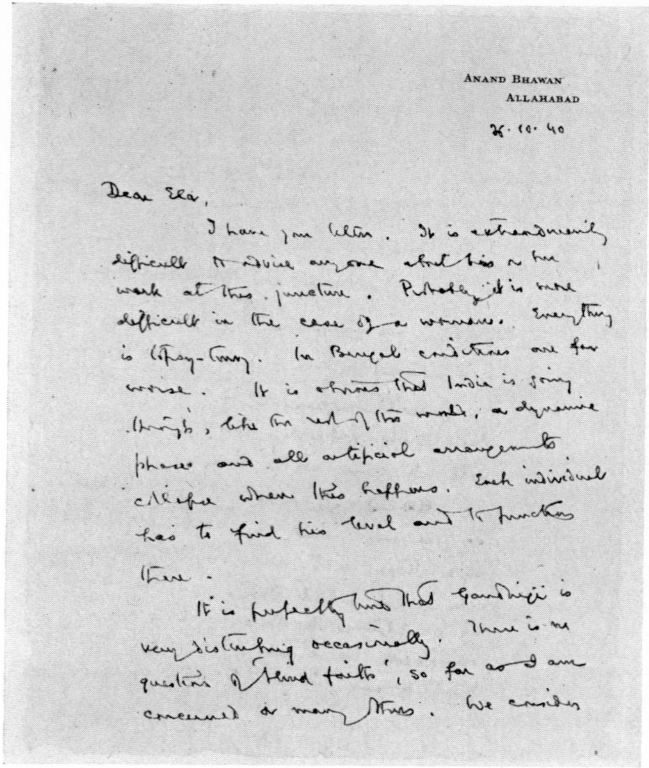

ANAND BHAWAN
ALLAHABAD

26.10.40

Dear Ela,

I have your letter. It is extraordinarily difficult to advise anyone about his or her work at this juncture. Probably it is more difficult in the case of a woman. Everything is topsy-turvy. In Bengal conditions are far worse. It is obvious that India is going through, like the rest of the world, a dynamic phase and all artificial arrangements collapse when this happens. Each individual has to find his level and to function there.

It is perfectly true that Gandhiji is very disturbing occasionally. There is no question of 'blind faith', so far as I am concerned or many others. We consider

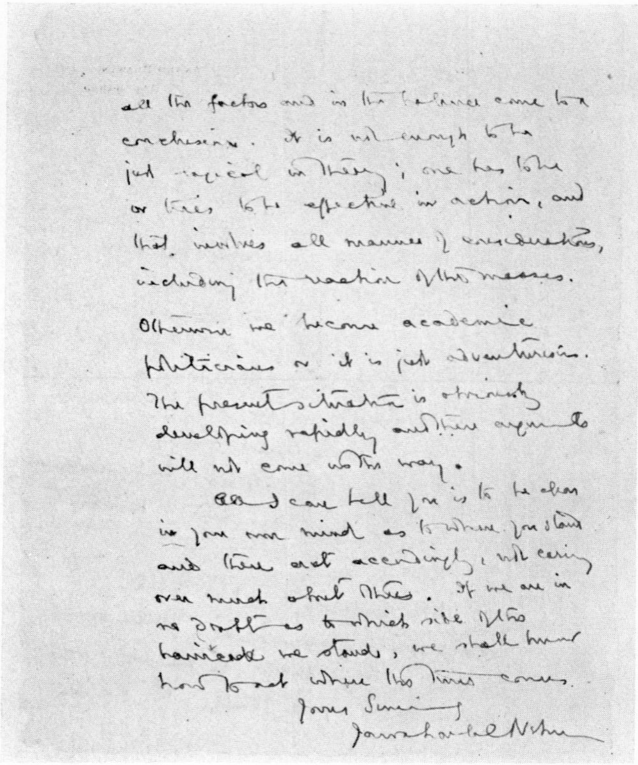

all the factors and in the balance come to a conclusion. It is not enough to be just logical in theory; one has to be or tries to be effective in action, and that involves all manner of considerations, including the reaction of the masses. Otherwise we become academic politicians or it is just adventurism. The present situation is obviously developing rapidly and these arguments will not come in the way.

All I can tell you is to be clear in your own mind as to where you stand and then act accordingly, not caring over much about others. If we are in no doubt as to which side of the barricade we stand, we shall know how to act when the time comes.

Yours sincerely
Jawaharlal Nehru

2 Letter from Jawaharlal Nehru to the author

On her return to her office, Mrs Gandhi made full enquiries into the situation and concluded regretfully that, since each faction had a case, the already partitioned province should be further divided into two states – Punjab for the Sikhs and Haryana for the Hindus. The one remaining complaint of the Hindus was that the Corbusier-designed town of Chandigarh remained the capital of Punjab; otherwise the aspirations of both groups were satisfied.

In West Bengal, too, there was serious trouble and the Congress Party had little or no power. There was anarchy – a constant battle between the various communist factions. Whatever the problem, the people of West Bengal had no time for the Congress Party, which had forfeited their trust. Indira Gandhi decided to explore the situation for herself. This was a courageous decision for, not only was the Congress Party unpopular, so were the Nehrus. The people of West Bengal felt that for twenty years nobody in central government had really cared what happened in West Bengal, least of all Jawaharlal Nehru. It was the one place where Nehru was no idol.

At the time when Indira was elected Prime Minister, West Bengal was undergoing an acute food shortage, due to the hoarding of food grains by some people with the purpose of unloading them on the Black Market. The Left Wing parties had called for a strike to paralyse Calcutta. Indira flew to Calcutta, but was prevented from speaking to the Left Wing leaders, because they had been arrested by the Congress-run State Government. She was bluntly critized by the Left Wing press for allowing bureaucracy to stand in her way, so she went back to Delhi. There was a strange atmosphere of impending doom in the city. She asked the Left Wing and Communist leaders to come to Delhi to talk with her. They told her that they wanted to stage a silent demonstration which would involve a walk through the city of Calcutta. Mrs Gandhi therefore instructed the Government not to provoke resistance, and the procession, led by writers and artists, subsequently passed peacefully through the streets of Calcutta. Her intervention made it possible for the Government-Communist dialogue to be resumed.

In the north-east of India, Indira was faced with action by the Naga and Mizo tribals, who were trying to effect a separatist movement. It was a full-scale rebellion, encouraged by the Christian missionaries, who had told the rebels that they should fight against a tyrannical Hindu domination. Mrs Gandhi flew out to the troubled areas, to try to open a peaceful dialogue, rather than using military force. Her action was firm but reasonable. It resulted ultimately in the expulsion of the Reverend Michael Scott from India.

After her election as Prime Minister, the first foreign envoy to call on her was Chester Bowles, the American Ambassador, bearing a letter of congratulation and an invitation to visit the United States from President Johnson: 'Let me offer you warm congratulations on your election and wish you every success as you assume the leadership of the world's largest democracy,' wrote Lyndon Johnson and continued: 'The relations between our two countries are firmly grounded on our common dedication to the principle of human dignity, human welfare, democratic institutions and peace. Under your leadership I look forward to broadening and deepening this community of interests and pledge our friendship and co-operation to this end. . . . Mrs Johnson and I remember with much pleasure our earlier meetings with you and look forward to seeing you again soon.'

In March 1966, Indira Gandhi paid her first visit to the United States as Prime Minister of India. She arrived by helicopter on the lawns of the White House in Washington and was welcomed by President and Mrs Johnson. Newspapers described her as looking small and delicate beside the President as she inspected the guard of honour. Apart from the formal functions that are inevitable on State visits, Indira Gandhi spoke informally to the President about the problems which India has to face. She spoke of crop failures, of bad monsoons, the poverty of the people and the vital necessity of raising agricultural output. She asked him to increase the aid he was giving her for these purposes. He promised an extra 500 million dollars out of the money India was paying America for shipments of food grains. The main topics for discussion were aid and Asian peace. But they also resolved not to intervene unduly in each other's foreign affairs. Without peace in Asia, India could not hope to progress as she wanted, Indira told President Johnson.

Indira's American visit was an unqualified success with the people as much as with the President and his wife. The *Washington Post* commented : 'No previous conference of heads of state in the time of the Johnson administration has accomplished so much for so many as have the President's parleys here with Mrs Indira Gandhi. . . . It turned out in short that she has been and intends to remain a modern-minded, undoctrinaire leader of India – not in our pockets, of course, but also not at our throats.'

Time Magazine commented that Mrs Gandhi was : 'a fiercely independent ruler, with a determination equal to President Johnson's own.'

In New York Indira gave a television interview, where she said quite frankly : 'It is true that there has been a feeling in India that over the Indo-Pakistan conflict (1965), Britain has not been very fair to India and this has created a little bit of tension. I think the United States showed greater understanding.'

It would appear that President Johnson had succeeded in winning Mrs Gandhi's confidence and goodwill. She now seemed willing to trust the motives of the US administration. This was a great achievement on the part of the US President. In turn, the President developed a high regard for Indira Gandhi.

Some press references to Indira, however, were unfavourable, the most restrained coming from the *Chicago Tribune*. It headlined its editorial 'An ungrateful suppliant' and said : 'It comes with little grace for Mrs Gandhi to criticize US policy in the Vietnam War and that even before she left our shores. Yet she did so on a television programme a few days after her talk with the President.' Quoting Mrs Gandhi the paper went on to say :

' "The US", said the Indian Prime Minister, "should not have extended the recent pause in bombings of North Vietnam." . . . The Prime Minister seems to have the same political myopia as her father, the late Jawaharlal Nehru. . . . Nobody in this country has ever suggested that India should become a satellite of the US, but we can suggest that Indian economy might benefit if that country should discard its socialist theories and pattern its economy after our private enterprise system.'

From Washington, Indira Gandhi went to England, France and Moscow. Her achievements in these countries were not spectacular. Moscow was not happy about her cordial relations with the USA and *Pravda* is quoted as having said that she had 'sold out' to the Americans. While she was in England, she received an honorary degree at Oxford; in France General de Gaulle promised his co-operation in her endeavours. Indira Gandhi's attitude towards Britain and the Wilson administration had hardened over the Labour Government's actions during the India-Pakistan War of 1965. This rather set the tone of her visit to London.

After Indira's visit to Washington and her success there, the Russians retaliated by making friendly overtures to Pakistan and, for the first time, agreed to sell her arms. Russian overtures to Pakistan were also prompted by the fact that China was already there on a friendly footing. Russia did not want to leave the field to China. She wished to stake her claim, but did not want totally to give up her friendly relations with India and in doing so encourage India's friendship with America who was also in Pakistan. Russia was prepared to continue her role as 'honest broker' to both Pakistan and India, as had been the case at Tashkent.

On her return home, Indira Gandhi took as her first task the relief of the acute drought situation in Bihar and in Uttar Pradesh. Here and elsewhere in the country, lack of food and inefficient distribution was resulting in strikes and *bandha* (closing down of all activity). These actions were not designed merely to embarrass the new Prime Minister, but were the only means the people had of drawing her attention to their problem. Parties joined together on these occasions. Indira knew the solution would not be easy to find, but that some action must be taken. The control of its food supplies was a prerogative of each State. Nevertheless, she asked Madras and Andhra to send some of their surplus food grains to neighbouring Kerala, where there was a great need. She also flew to Kerala to assess the situation for herself, and assured the scarcity States that the Central Government would try its utmost to help them.

Mrs Gandhi had stepped into her job at the most critical time in India's post-independence history, especially as she was not expected to succeed in any field. Her own party gave her no support; its leaders wanted to follow a *laissez-faire* policy which was bound to show her as inept. During the last few years, the Central Government had become a prisoner of its own Constitution; it had grown weak and was very much at the mercy of the individual States which under the Constitution were autonomous. When the Constitution had been made, the Chief Ministers of the States had been strong men who could command solid backing from the people. During the past ten years politics had deteriorated to a condition where nepotism, self-interest, corruption and strong-arm tactics were rife. The standard of living had gone down; unemployment had risen each year and jobs were obtained either by favour or bribery.

The ordinary people were sick of it all. Congress rule was a by-word for derision. This was the state of affairs inherited by Indira Gandhi and she could count on very little help from her colleagues to better the Party's reputation or strengthen her own.

By the month of May, it had become clear that there would again be monsoon failure with resultant drought. The Prime Minister had now to prevent what had been scarcity becoming a famine. The delegates at the Party session decided that the existing regional control of food should be abolished. Mrs Gandhi would have liked to do so. It was not that there was no food in the country – there were States that had surplus food grain. But here she came up against the autonomy of the States. Even the

President had no power to commandeer surplus food grains for distribution to the scarcity areas. Distribution itself was no problem; the army had offered its services for this purpose. There was no way of reaching a solution unless the States were willing to co-operate – a Constitution had been made and its provisions could not be ignored.

Indira Gandhi brought some relief by using up precious foreign exchange: she bought wheat from Australia, the USA and Canada. (The rice-growing Asian countries were self-sufficient and their surpluses could not match India's needs.) Then the Prime Minister resolved that if she wanted to be returned at the next election, she must concentrate on agriculture; she would get high-yielding seed from Japan and the rice-growing countries.

She immediately gave top priority to agriculture and the digging of wells. India's economists had concentrated on industrialization at the expense of agriculture. Indira decided that no more steel plants should be built and that an all-out effort must be made to ensure that famine was prevented. To this end, high-yielding crop seeds were brought from Japan and Canada and distributed to the peasants. Fertilizers and water were made available. Tax concessions were made to farmers. Restrictions were placed on the amount of farming acreage an individual might buy; but those who wanted to evade the laws bought land in plots in the names of various members of their families. Townspeople rushed to invest their hoarded wealth – described as 'black money' because it had not been declared to the Inland Revenue – in agriculture in the villages. It was not all carried through in the most ethical of ways, perhaps, but the 'Grow More Food' campaign had certainly begun in earnest.

The rank and file Congress Party members were tired of the emergency powers curbing civil liberties which had existed since 1962. Indira Gandhi disliked this as much as they did, but the Chief Ministers of various States said that there would be no law and order if she lifted these. On this point she suffered her second defeat.

By this time the Congress Parliamentary Party was beginning

to wonder if after all it had not made a mistake in choosing Indira Gandhi. Followers of Morarji Desai fanned this feeling and had been doing so assiduously during her absence abroad, brief though it was. The extra aid she had secured from President Johnson of 500 million dollars was severely criticized by the Left as representing a sell-out to the USA.

The magnitude of the burdens that had been calmly shifted on to her shoulders was appreciated by nobody. Those who should have and could have helped sat back and watched to see how it would all work out. Even Kamraj, busy with his own problems in Madras State, where a new anti-Congress, anti-Hindi party was fast growing, had become less friendly towards Indira. Her independent nature had proved very clearly that she would not be his pawn.

In Delhi, the Jan Sangh, a communal Hindu organization which had some following there, started a movement to prohibit cow slaughter. They knew very well that the control of agriculture was the prerogative of the States, and to embarrass Mrs Gandhi they carried on their agitation among the illiterate Hindu masses, who did not know that the Prime Minister had no jurisdiction in the matter. In a rather macabre finale, a number of naked, ash-smeared, so-called Hindu holy men, armed with tridents and axes, tried to invade the Lok-Sabha, smashed down government buildings and set fire to the houses of officials. Most of them were beggars who, with a little money to encourage them, were willing to act the part of *sadhus*. It was some time before the police were called out, as the Home Minister was the communal, Gulzarilal Nanda. Finally, the police appeared and the crowd was quickly dispersed. Indira Gandhi was forced to dismiss Nanda and replace him with Y. B. Chavan, until then the Defence Minister. The Congress had been pressing her to reshuffle the Cabinet and she would have liked to have replaced one or two other ministers, whose appointments dated from her predecessor's time. But she was unable to do so, even though they were obstructive to her policies.

The year Indira had been in office had confirmed what she knew when she took office: that she had been selected for the purpose of winning the 1967 election for the Congress Party. The Party knew, and she knew, that only Indira Gandhi could win power back for the Congress Party. The unpopularity of the Party and the trend of the country towards communism could only be stemmed with great difficulty. She was also quite well aware that she was expected to 'keep the seat warm' for the chosen candidate of the Party bosses, and step down gracefully. This too she determined not to do. If she was going to win the elections for the Party, she would keep her position.

The people – the ordinary people – of India gave Indira the love and loyalty they had given to her father. Since the 'thirties he had been the idol of the nation and 90 per cent of the Indian people had believed in him. Jawaharlal Nehru had done much that the masses of India had not understood; they could not know what effect his actions would have on their lives, but they had believed that he would not do anything that would hurt them or their interests. They felt the same about his daughter, who had set herself to cultivate the masses during the months before her. 'The people of India love me,' Indira said, and made that her capital, which she determined to convert to riches.

Indira had inherited from her father an enormous capacity for work. No task which was expected of her was too difficult or too arduous. She travelled vast distances, she spoke to groups of politicians in each State, she addressed mammoth rallies. State governments understood her language, they realized that from her they would get support and guidance. The situation at home, however, did not improve. Industry suffered and unemployment of the educated grew. Young engineers who a year before could have been assured of employment, now formed the largest section of the unemployed. Consumer goods were scarce. There was an iron and steel surplus but these commodities were being exported rather than being used at home to build up factories for the manufacture of consumer goods.

During 1966-67, while Indira served what one could describe as her apprenticeship as Prime Minister, she made a number of mistakes and often there were rumours that the Congress Party would drop her. Once she even offered to resign, but Kamraj knew that Indira was the Congress Party's only hope, now that a new party of the rich and those on the extreme Right had been formed, hoping to make inroads into Congress support. Indira knew this too. She built up her own defence; she went on increasing her contacts with the people, whom everybody else thought could be forced, bribed or 'worked on' in other ways.

The new party was called *Swatantra* – 'different', 'separate' or 'isolationist'. The latter the members certainly were, for the party was composed of the rich minority – princes, merchant princes, landlords, Right Wing intellectuals. The princes, on India's independence, had been fairly and compassionately treated, but many of their privileges had been taken away and their personal incomes somewhat reduced and the money ploughed back into the State. Absolutism was abolished and there was democratic legislation in all the States. These people rushed to join the Swatantra Party, intending to keep intact their still high incomes and existing privileges. The initiative for the formation of the party came from a veteran nationalist, C. Rajagopalachariar, who had been a leading member of the Congress Party, had fought for India's independence and had become independent India's Governor General. Then, in his eighties, he felt the need to break down the monolithic Congress Party and make a clear demarcation between the various movements within it. There already existed the Hindu Communal Party, the Communist Party and the Congress Party. These, he felt, could not provide a platform for the rich Right Wing, who had an equal right to be represented in Parliament. Therefore he started the Swatantra Party as its President, hoping to wean members away from the Congress Party.

Another new party emerged in Madras, in the south. It was popularly known as DMK, or Dravida Mundhra Khagazam, and was formed largely to resist the domination of the Hindi-speaking people from the north. The Communist Party split into two separate parties, one of which was Moscow-orientated, the other China-orientated.

Problems within the country were tremendous. Failure of the monsoon, food scarcity and food riots, language frictions between peoples and States, tribal rebellions in the hill areas of Assam in the north-east, an unrealistic five-year plan, the industrial slump, growing economic distress and unemployment : all these problems were entered on the debit side of Indira's stewardship, although they had all been present before she took over. Critics were numerous. Her own kith and kin were among the most vociferous. Some Congress Party followers maintained that she was not strong enough. She was blamed for selecting unsuitable advisers. People did not realize that only a very strong character with faith and knowledge as to the nature and extent of her following would have persisted.

President Nasser of Egypt and President Tito of Yugoslavia came to New Delhi to meet Mrs Gandhi. They were concerned about the American bombings of North Vietnam. They felt that the uncommitted nations should try to intervene. After a great deal of discussion, a joint communiqué was issued, calling upon the USA to discontinue bombing raids and condemning its actions. This may be regarded as the first breach in Indo-US relations. America was extremely displeased at the action taken. She now discovered that Indira had meant what she said when she returned from America : that she believed in non-alignment and was an independent ruler. It will be recalled that a few months before, after her favourable reception in America, she had been accused by some of her colleagues of having sold out to the USA. But Indira had not signed the joint communiqué under any pressure or influence from anybody. She, as Prime Minister of India, had already protested to the USA about the indiscriminate bombing that had been inflicted on North Vietnam.

In the meantime, with only a few months left before the General Election, she started an electioneering tour of India, concentrating particularly on the areas where the Congress Party was not popular. Her father's constituency of Phulpur, near Allahabad, she could have taken for herself, but she left it for her aunt, Mrs Pandit. She herself stood from Rae Bareilly, also in Uttar Pradesh, her husband Feroze's old constituency. In spite of the personal attacks she had suffered from Mrs Pandit and her family, she appeared on the platform at Phulpur to speak for her aunt. The daughter of Jawaharlal Nehru could not fail to impress the voters there.

Indira Gandhi went to Orissa and spoke at mass meetings in the capital of that State, at one of which some anti-Congress demonstrators hurled stones at her. She was hit on the nose and sustained a fracture. Holding a handkerchief to her bleeding face, she retorted : 'This is not an insult to me, but as Prime Minister it is a grave insult to the country I represent, which is also your country.' From there, in spite of her injury, she went to Madras, where the new party, DMK, was making great headway. Indira tried to rally Congress supporters, reminding them of the brave days of the Congress Party when it wrested independence from Britain. In West Bengal also, Indira Gandhi tried to rally Congress supporters, even though she knew that the Congress leaders by their own corruption and nepotism had destroyed the Party's chances of success.

At Jaipur, which was a stronghold of the Swatantra Party, where the Maharani herself was standing for the Lok-Sabha, Indira was again attacked and demonstrators and hecklers tried to break up her meetings. Always calm, as she had shown herself at all times, a spark of the Nehru temper flashed out in Jaipur, when she said to the hecklers : 'I am not going to be shouted down. I know who is behind these demonstrations and I know how to make myself heard. I am going to do some plain speaking today. Your slogans do not change your past history. What were the Jan Sangh adherents doing while the country was under foreign rule? Go and ask your Maharaja and Maharani how many wells they dug for their people, how many roads they constructed, while they lived in luxury at the cost of the people. If you, the people, will look for their achievements while they were your rulers, you will find a big zero.' That silenced the hecklers.

Indira carried on her campaign all over the country, for the States as well as the central legislature, to put the Congress Party back into power. If she was to continue as Prime Minister, as she had every intention of doing, she wanted the people's mandate.

The General Election was held in February, 1967. Indira was returned with a large majority, while the older members of the Congress Party were mostly defeated, except for Morarji Desai, who won with a good majority. The most significant defeat was that of Kamraj Nadar in a Madras constituency, by an unknown young man supporting DMK. The Congress Party was returned to the Central Government with a reduced majority of 55 per cent where it had been 75 per cent. This reduction showed the extent of the Right Wing parties' success, and how far the electorate's confidence in the Congress Party had been shaken. The Congress Party lost in eight States. Two were dominated by the Communist Parties and coalitions ruled the others, except for Madras, which was won by the DMK.

At the centre, Indira's leadership should have been unquestioned. She had been returned by the mandate of the people, not by the influence or choice of any one person. But once more Morarji Desai refused to stand down; he was the only member of the Syndicate who had won back his seat. The Parliamentary Party had once more to make a choice. Kamraj Nadar again became a tactician, trying to unify and conciliate the candidates. Morarji Desai should withdraw from his claim to the Prime Ministership in favour of Indira, if she would accept him as Deputy Prime Minister and Home Minister. Indira refused to allot the Home portfolio to him, but agreed to make him Deputy Prime Minister and Finance Minister. Finally Morarji Desai agreed, presumably thinking that since he was not out of the Cabinet he might, by intrigue, yet realize his ultimate ambition if he were on the spot.

Once again, on 12 March, 1967, Indira was elected Leader of the Congress Party and drove to the President's house, where she was asked to form a government as India's Prime Minister. Thus Indira had another five years in which to accomplish all she could for the people of India. Their faith in her had returned her to office and she was determined they would not be disappointed. With only 55 per cent of the seats to the credit of the Congress Party in Lok-Sabha, it would not be easy, but she knew that her policies would attract new allies.

7

Prime Minister

When in 1967 Indira Gandhi became Prime Minister again she occupied an uneasy seat of power. Very few people realized, or wanted to recognize, her potentialities. They still looked upon her as a reflection of the Nehru charisma. During this period Mrs Pandit resigned her seat in Parliament to express her disapproval of her niece's (Mrs Gandhi's) policies. 'She is as calm as the waters of the ocean,' somebody recently said of Indira Gandhi's temperament, but few in 1967 realized that a dynamic force lay within the depths of that ocean.

Morris-Jones, in a well-documented work,* comments on Indira as she appeared in 1967: 'Indira Gandhi was less than dominant when she came to the political throne in 1966 – a situation reflected in the revival after 16 years of the office of Deputy Prime Minister which had to be given to her rival Morarji Desai and, although she largely escaped blame for the shock to Congress fortunes of the 1967 elections, her position remained difficult. Indeed it worsened in 1969 which brought about by the end of the year the split in the Party.' This writer seems to be unaware of the real reason why Kamraj had sponsored her as Prime Minister in 1966, the year preceding the General Election; it was that only the daughter of Jawaharlal Nehru could retrieve the prestige lost by the Congress Party and

* Morris-Jones, W. H., *Government and Politics of India* (Hutchinson, 1967).

102

win the election. If Shastri had been alive, it is doubtful whether, without help from Indira Gandhi, he could have secured even the 50 per cent majority which Congress won. She had no illusions as to why the choice of Prime Ministership had fallen on her in 1966 and that she was expected merely to be a fill-in.

An interesting affair now came to light. It was alleged that Morarji Desai's son had been using information obtained from his father's files for his own interests with certain industrialists. This was for Morarji Desai, who prided himself on his honesty and morality, a great set-back. Lok-Sabha members wanted him to resign. It was the Prime Minister who stepped forward to his defence and maintained that he was free from involvement. What his son had done did not affect him and he would remain as the Deputy Prime Minister. After his enmity towards her, her gesture was considered to be one of great magnanimity. It is also true that by this one act Mrs Gandhi increased her own prestige and ensured that Morarji Desai had no chance of becoming Prime Minister.

One of Mrs Gandhi's first actions as Prime Minister was to conduct an enquiry into the activities of foreign cultural organizations which were suspected of acting as a cloak for undesirable political activity. It was made clear to foreign powers that while a cultural mission could be attached to an embassy, such an organization would not be allowed to function where there was no diplomatic mission. The activities of various American Foundations also came under scrutiny, together with the irregular disbursement of sums from funds accrued in rupees as payment for PL 480 wheat aid from the US. The reports were unfavourable and American Foundations, such as the Asia Foundation, had to move on to Hong-Kong and other places.

The schism within the Congress Party had begun even in the days when Jawaharlal Nehru dominated Indian politics with his dream of building a socialist India. On the achievement of independence Gandhi had wisely advised the dissolution of the Congress Party as it stood, and that groups of individuals should divide into parliamentary parties as in other democratic countries.

He was fully aware of the variations within the Congress Party which must in the end lead to its collapse, since the factions were united only by the theme of independence. Even in his lifetime, Gandhi's two stalwarts, Nehru and Vallabhai Patel, very rarely agreed. Patel supported the industrialists, who financed the Congress Party, and the princes; Nehru was the expert on foreign relations, always thinking of how best to create the nucleus of his socialist India. It was Patel and Lord Mountbatten who created a favourable charter for the Indian princes. Mountbatten sold the idea to Nehru, leaving intact the privileges and substantial privy purses which Nehru's daughter was to nullify twenty-five years later. The majority of the old guard did not agree with any of Nehru's policies but some of them like Govind Vallabh Pant and Abul Kalam Azad supported him loyally, and Gandhi's assassination healed the breach between the Congress leaders, even between Nehru and Patel. They all knew that it was only Nehru who could defend the Congress Party from the inroads of the communists whose leaders, in spite of having been imprisoned, won large numbers of seats in the State and Central legislatures in 1952.

As Nehru grew older, the differences between him and his colleagues, younger and ambitious, resentful of the ageing Prime Minister's dominance, came more and more to the surface. But his colleagues continued to dominate the party caucus until Indira Gandhi, as President of the Congress Party in 1959, forced retirement on some of them and filled the gaps with younger men and women. She tried to make the Congress a forward looking party. When Kamraj became President, in an effort to revive Congress prestige, he suggested that some of the older and noted members in ministerial positions should resign in order to devote themselves to party work. This policy did not succeed, for a taste of power had made them ambitious, and they soon pushed themselves back into power. It must be considered Nehru's failure that he was not able to remove the old guard in favour of young and able men.

During the All India Congress Committee sessions of 1966,

after a keen debate, it was established that India was, in gradual stages, to become a socialist state. Several resolutions were passed which were to have far-reaching consequences in the 'seventies. These were : the abolition of the privileges and privy purses of the Indian princes; nationalization of all insurance and nationalization of the larger Indian banks. This was the first defeat for the old guard, but while their influence lasted in the States and at the centre, these resolutions would remain nothing more than pious thoughts for the Minute book. Who could ever be strong enough to apply them in reality, if the old guard opposed it? Their only misgiving was a feeling that Indira Gandhi had either to be controlled or deposed. They got their chance in 1969 when Dr Zakir Hussein, the President of India, died and a new President had to be elected. Usually the process was painless, with the electoral college agreeing unanimously on the majority party's choice; if there were another candidate, he really had no chance. Such opposition was usually in the nature of a protest by one of the opposition parties.

When the nomination for the President came up, Indira Gandhi's enemies saw that there might be a chance of deposing her if the President's powers could be increased. This could only be achieved by changing the Constitution with a two-thirds majority. Their man at the top was Sanjeeva Reddi, very much a man of the Syndicate, and personally hostile to Indira Gandhi. Indira, as leader of the Party, did not oppose the choice until she began to understand the real reasons behind the choice of Sanjeeva Reddi. With a 50 per cent majority in the Congress, allied with the other Right Wing groups, her opponents would not find it difficult to get the two-thirds majority required to change the Constitution and create powers for the President in the American style. The Prime Minister would then be redundant.

Indira Gandhi resolved to fight it out. She took the unprecedented step of nominating a rival candidate from the Congress Party – V. V. Giri, a well known labour leader from the days of India's fight for independence, and she canvassed for him. On 9 August, 1969, Giri was elected President of India and her first major political victory had fallen to Indira. The wrath of the Syndicate was terrible and the Working Committee was split. Mrs Gandhi dismissed two junior ministers known to be Syndicate supporters and she sent out, as leader of the Party, a notice to the AICC to elect a new President in place of Nijalingappa, who had eased out one of her supporters from the Working Committee so that he would have a majority of one in any decision. (Indira had ten members on the Working Committee and Nijalingappa had eleven.) At this point Indira Gandhi and other rebellious members were expelled from the Congress Party. She, who had been so restrained in her grief when her father died, wept at this blow struck at her by those who claimed to represent the organization built up by her grandfather and father, but she accepted the challenge and fought back. She emerged with her ten Working Committee members, more than half the members of the AICC, three-quarters of the Congress MPs and most of the Chief Ministers of the State legislatures. The 84-year old monolithic party had cracked. It was ended. Indira said : 'My Congress is *the* Congress. I don't know what the other is called and I do not care. People have shown twice over that they want me, and with their help I will go on.' Her following from the Party was known as Congress R or the Ruling Congress Party. The other was known as Congress O or the Organizational Congress.

Although the old guard tried to fasten the blame for the breakup on Indira, it was recognized that much earlier there had been two Congress parties in West Bengal, Orissa and Kerala, because of dissatisfaction with the Tammany Hall tactics of the All India Congress Party. Indira Gandhi told a critical press conference : 'It existed [the danger of a split] in my father's time and, in fact, during the last three years of his life it was acute. That was why the Kamraj Plans and all these things came into being.' Indira Gandhi was asked what would happen now after her expulsion : would there be a stable peace or the peace of the grave? To this she replied : 'When the question of unity was asked, I said that it should not be a unity for suicide. I did not mean suicide for myself or for a particular group. I meant for the Congress as a whole. We all know that the people have been moving away from the Congress, either openly forming other parties or just deciding to sit back and not function and not work. Many of the old and sincere workers have been thus pushed aside, and at the same time we are not attracting young people as we should. Therefore, unless we can give a new image of the Congress to the people, the future of the Congress is not as bright as it should be.'

An interesting fact emerged during this 'battle of the giants'; it was that about half a dozen card-holding members of the Communist Party of India tore up their party cards and joined Congress R. Three of them are now in Ministerial positions.

Mrs Gandhi was not against such a 'change of heart' nor was she afraid that, once in, the Communists would be able to push her out. She knew that she needed the support of the Left Wing parties in the changes she wanted to bring about. Many of her proposals could raise violent storms, but she knew that they would be on such lines that the Communist Party of India must support them or run contrary to all its socialist ideals.

Feeling more secure in her office of Prime Minister, Mrs Gandhi now set about forming her own pattern for governmental procedure. She began to get younger men and women into key positions. Of the old comrades, a few still remained with her – Jagjivan Ram whom she made President of Congress R and Y. B. Chavan who became the Home Minister; the Foreign portfolio went to the Sikh representative, Sardar Swaran Singh, with the younger, astute and experienced T. N. Kaul as Foreign Secretary. The young Maharaja of Kashmir, who preferred to drop his title and be known as Dr Karan Singh, became Minister for Tourism, and Dinesh Singh took on the Industries portfolio. Mrs Gandhi herself temporarily kept the administration of Finance as part of her duties. But a vital and far-reaching change was in her elevation of the position of the Prime Minister's Secretariat, where the principal executive holds a position superior to the Cabinet Secretary. P. N. Haksar, the Principal Secretary, is a Kashmiri and a lawyer from Allahabad, who entered foreign service when India became independent. The Secretariat is closer to the Prime

Minister than the Cabinet. Haksar's counsel, influence, good judgement and unquestioned loyalty to the Prime Minister have helped her to follow a judicious and confident policy.

Many of Indira Gandhi's critics wondered why she should have selected Jagjivan Ram to be President of her Congress Party. There were at that time many allegations against him that he had failed to pay his income tax, and so on. But she knew that almost three-quarters of a million votes of the Harijans, from whom Jagjivan Ram sprang, were very much at his command. He was a valuable ally for Indira Gandhi in the game of politics. In the same way Y. B. Chavan's influence in Maharashtra was not to be ignored. He was a strong man and in her government he would strengthen her position, particularly in Maharashtra. In other hands he could be set up as an opponent against her. Had Chavan given up his ambitions so easily? It is not likely. He joined Indira Gandhi thinking to use his position for his own advantage, but he had underestimated, as had so many others, her political acumen. Such underestimations were always in her favour; her political moves were not flaunted and always took her enemies by surprise.

At this period, perhaps to show their contempt for a woman prime minister and knowing this would please the press lords, journalists coined the phrase 'Kitchen Cabinet' to represent some advisers and ministers who were close to her in her councils. Where would a woman meet her fellow conspirators except in a kitchen, which is her domain? It is doubtful if this disturbed Indira Gandhi at all. She went on with her work and the plans for a socialist India which she had set afoot.

The life assurance industry had been nationalized during Pandit Nehru's premiership, following Feroze Gandhi's exposure of grave abuses in that sphere, in which Finance Department officials had been implicated. Now the Government of India gave notice that by 1972 all general insurance would be nationalized. Compensation was promised but those who had drawn fat profits for years from their companies were naturally displeased and hoped that by 1972 Indira Gandhi would no longer be Prime

Minister. The next General Election was due in February or March, 1972.

In the summer of 1968 Indira Gandhi announced the nationalization of the large Indian-owned banks, which comprised fourteen of the scheduled banks. She spoke to the people over All India Radio to tell the country what nationalization was, what was about to happen and why. She reminded people that the Congress Party had only recently taken a resolution to this effect. As early as 1954 Parliament had taken a decision that India would plan for a socialist pattern of society. She said that to achieve this: 'Control over the commanding heights of the economy is necessary particularly in a poor country. . . . Ours is an ancient country but a young democracy which has to remain ever vigilant to prevent the domination of the few over the social, economic and political systems. Banks play a vital role in the functioning of any economy. To those who have money to spare, banks are the custodians of their savings on which a good return can be earned by wise and effective management. To the millions of small farmers, artisans and other self-employed persons, a bank can be a source of credit, which is the very basis of any effort to improve their meagre economic lot. . . .'

The objectives of nationalizing the bigger banks were, firstly, the removal of control by a few, then provision of adequate credit for agriculture, small industry and exports. Bank management would become a profession and there would be a new class of entrepreneurs to whom credit would be extended. This was now controlled by the big commercial houses owning the banks so that the little man got no chance to start up small-scale industries. Bank staff would be adequately trained and reasonable terms of service would be offered. 'The present situation,' the Prime Minister commented, 'leaves much to be desired. Nationalization is necessary for the speedy achievement of these objectives.'

A bill for the nationalization of fourteen of the seventy-four scheduled banks was introduced into Parliament in July 1969 as the 'Acquisition and Transfer of Undertakings Bill'. After a detailed debate, in which the Prime Minister took part, the Bill was passed. The Prime Minister outlined what she considered to be the role of banks in a developing country whose objective was the achievement of a socialist society.

Banks were at the time positioned mostly in urban areas or local small towns, so that the agriculturist in the villages had perforce to bank his savings in urban banks. Deposits from rural areas were thus being used as a means of financing urban industries rather than being ploughed back into agricultural development. This, Mrs Gandhi felt, had to be remedied; the farmer must have banks within reach, so that new entrepreneurs could utilize them for development within that area.

A natural question which arose was why foreign banks were not being nationalized. It was made quite clear that all foreign banks were within the jurisdiction of the Government of India but that at the moment they served a useful purpose for exporters, who presented their bills of lading, etc., through the relevant bank. Thus they were not impairing the economy of the country but rather helping its export trade.

The banking houses were prepared for a trial of strength with the Government and jointly appealed to the Supreme Court; the judgement was given in their favour with two judges of the full bench dissenting. The Prime Minister asked the President to promulgate an Ordinance by which the Bill passed in Parliament became a law of the land.

The banks remained autonomous but their employees were now government servants. The managers were renamed custodians – custodians of the public's money. Speaking to the custodians in September 1969, the Prime Minister said : 'A complaint has been voiced that with nationalization, operations of banks will always be swayed by political considerations. I do not know what these critics have in mind . . . banks are too closely linked with the development of the economy to remain entirely uninfluenced by the needs of the political situation. The political situation in our country today demands that banking facilities should be extended in an increasing measure to the backward areas, to

agriculture, to small-scale industry and so on, and perhaps banking operations should be enforced by a larger social purpose.'

After the achievement of her first major reformatory step,
Indira Gandhi found that her opponents in Parliament had closed
their ranks and were determined to do battle in every major
change which was brought to the Lok-Sabha. Her next innova-
tion was a minor one but it was bad political judgement to
introduce it then, knowing the mood and character of the Opposition.

There were a few people left over from the bureaucratic British
days of the Indian Civil Service. These men had served the
British well; when the transfer of power came they accepted the
situation and began to serve their Indian masters with efficiency,
if not exactly with love. They knew the rules of government and
were extremely useful to the new regime. Their salary scales were
guaranteed together with all the privileges they had enjoyed
under British rule, down to what was known in those days as
'home' leave or leave in Britain. The younger generation that
grew up in the Indian Administrative Service did not enjoy any
such privileges, neither was their salary scale comparable. These
were able young men and women and within a generation they
began to resent the differences in working conditions. The makers
of modern and independent India had argued that the ICS cadre
would not last more than twenty-five years, after which only the
new administrators would remain. But the 'old school tie' corps
lingered, along with many out-of-date ideas and tendencies; they
seemed too prone to foreign influences, and not wholly orientated
towards Free India's interests. Mrs Gandhi sought to level up
the differences between the old and the new by curtailing the
privileges of the old ICS, which could only be done through
Parliament, since these were all arrangements made at the time
of the transfer of power from Britain.

The Prime Minister was unable to get the measure through,
however; she lost the motion and for the time being went no
further with it. She felt that there were weightier measures she

meant to get through Parliament first, and time would assist her in reducing inequalities. The setback was only temporary.

Among the greatest remaining inequalities were those concerning the Indian princes, who persisted in maintaining a feudal regime. These princes had been left with privy purses which were paid out of the State Government's treasury. The grant of Privy purses to the rulers was a sort of *quid pro quo* (from the British) for the surrender by them of all their ruling powers and for the dissolution of their States. Apart from this, the rulers were also allowed to retain certain private property and the personal rights and privileges which they had enjoyed under British rule. In fact, even after twenty-five years, the princes were not within the jurisdiction of the country's law which governed all other inhabitants of India – rich and poor alike. They maintained many feudal privileges such as the legal right to commit murder without fear of arrest or trial. It is incredible that a Government thinking in terms of democracy and socialism should have allowed such privileges to survive. What appears quite incomprehensible is that this was incorporated within the Constitution of India, and could only be altered or corrected by a 75 per cent majority in Parliament. Lord Mountbatten had considerable influence over what should go into the Constitution, particularly regarding protection for the princes, the most favoured lackeys of British imperialism in India.

Mrs Gandhi in her approach to socialism thought much about the differences separating the princes from the rest of the people of India. India was a very poor country where if one got two meals a day one was lucky. Whereas the princes were able, if they pleased, to consume foreign liquor purchased at special prices; their incomes per year were well over Rs. 100,000.† At the time of the Congress settlement at the time of independence the privy purse was fixed so that if the income of the State was Rs. 15,000,000 then the privy purse would be valued at Rs. 130,000 which was 20 per cent less than under British rule.

† The exchange rate is at present about 19 rupees to the English £.

There were 554 princely States whose rulers still enjoyed untaxed, unearned means, but of these about 450 had revenues less than Rs. 15,000,000.

But the above-mentioned figures and rules did not apply to the following eleven States, the privy purses for which were fixed for the rulers arbitrarily.

State	Privy purse per year (all untaxed)
Hyderabad	Rs. 430,000
Baroda	Rs. 265,000
Mysore	Rs. 260,000
Gwalior	Rs. 250,000
Jaipur	Rs. 180,000
Travancore	Rs. 175,000
Jodhpur	Rs. 170,000
Bikaner	Rs. 170,000
Patiala	Rs. 170,000
Indore	Rs. 150,000
Bhopal	Rs. 110,000

In the case of these rulers it was postulated that these amounts were to apply only during their lifetime and that their successors would get such amounts as the Government of the day thought fit, and in any case not more than Rs. 100,000. There were some rulers in Orissa and in Saurashtra whose estates were so small that they were put together to make a bigger whole and get an adequate income.

In dollars or sterling the amounts involved are not great, although the rulers had private property as well. Why then did Mrs Gandhi decide to denude them of their rights and privileges? Because in a country as poor as India which is aiming at socialism, it is inconceivable to allow a section of the people to exist outside the law of the land, a group, moreover, who did not need to be productive or add to the country's resources since they could live on an unearned income.

The Government entered into discussions with the Concord of Princes to see if a change of affairs could be brought about amicably. Some of the rulers, for instance the Gaekwar of Baroda, adopted a soft line but others, with customary arrogance, opted for fierce opposition.

In December 1970 Indira Gandhi's Government introduced proposals for legislation to amend the relevant clauses of the Constitution, for the abolition of privy purses and privileges and the de-recognition of the princes. News reporters described the scene in the visitors' gallery, packed with silk- and chiffon-clad ladies exuding expensive perfumes, mingling with the *canaille* they despised. In the Lower House, Lok-Sabha, with the help of independent small parties and Left Wing parties, Mrs Gandhi secured her two-thirds majority. But it still had to be endorsed by the Upper House or Rajya-Sabha. There, Indira Gandhi lost her motion by one vote only. This was unexpected, but the President had, under the Constitution, the power to de-recognize any prince. Now, with one signature, he de-recognized all 550 of them.

The princes, however, felt that they were fighting for their lives. Mrs Gandhi was bringing in her revolution the non-violent way, and was in fact protecting their lives against the wrath of their subjects, who would rouse themselves sooner or later against the injustices and brutalities inflicted upon them. But the princes engaged themselves a good lawyer and went to the Supreme Court. They won their case against the Government and hoped to live on their unearned incomes for the rest of their lives.

Mrs Gandhi had suffered a major setback, but she said little about it in public and appeared to have accepted the defeat. In private she was as calm as in public, but she was heard to say: 'Give me another six months – it is not a lot to delay.' People felt this was wishful thinking. The princes were confident and slept easy. Indira Gandhi's opponents were jubilant. At last, they said, she had overstepped herself.

Meanwhile, three new States had been born in India. The Sikhs, as we have seen, had been given their homeland. The other two were tribal States on the northern borders of Assam. Here, the hill people were totally different from the plainsmen of Assam. The State of Meghalaya came into being to fulfil the aspirations of the people of the Khasi and Jaintia Hills. Arunalaya is the State lying near the State of Manipur and is the home of the Mizo tribe, who, like the Nagas, have been a trial to the military and civil authorities on the North-East Frontier. But today, with a State of their own within the Indian Union, the tribesmen are happy. They receive from the centre the same assistance as any of the other States do.

The 'Green Revolution', to make India self-sufficient in food, was another of Indira Gandhi's top priorities. India is dependent greatly on her monsoons for the success of her crops, but 1968-70 were good years and wheat was almost in surplus. A buffer stock had been built up to meet any future scarcity. Rice was still short in some States which were predominantly rice-eating, but high-yielding grains had been imported from Japan and were expected to make an impact on the rice shortfall. Success in fighting food shortages was still largely dependent on seasonal variation. But the Government could say that India was not a scarcity country. All manner of incentives such as tax relief had been offered to farmers to make up for the neglect which, under the pressure of industrialization, agriculture had suffered. Farmers were helped by fertilizers, the loaning of tractors and the channelling of water from canals for irrigation. The 'Green Revolution' was on its way. Although a ceiling had been put on the possession of agricultural land, to prevent the development of agricultural estates and the deprivation of those who already possessed farms, small though they might be, abuses were bound to creep in. One such practice was that whereby small pieces of land were bought in the names of various members of the same family which together amounted to a large estate; these were often controlled by city merchants. But the Prime Minister's problem was first of all to increase the output of food – the attendant problems could be dealt with later.

On 28 December, 1970 Indira Gandhi took her opponents by

surprise by declaring that there would be an immediate General
Election for the Lok-Sabha and most of the States' legislatures.
Those for Kerala and West Bengal would be held later owing to
troubled conditions in those two States.

8

Garibi Hatao

Having announced a mid-term poll for Lok-Sabha, Indira Gandhi took as her slogan 'Garibi Hatao' or Banish Poverty. This was the summary of her party's election manifesto. She dissolved Parliament and on 27 December, over All India Radio, made her announcement to the country that there would be a General Election in February/March 1971. The Election Commissioner then took over the arrangements for the election. Mrs Gandhi informed the press on 29 December at a press conference that the Government was one which had had the full confidence of Parliament. Until the next one was elected, it had full powers to administer law and order in the country and to conduct the country's affairs as before.

Mrs Gandhi's bold decision had surprised friends and enemies alike. There had been no motion of No Confidence, and they could not understand why Indira was going to the country for a fresh mandate when she still had the full confidence of Parliament. The press asked her why she had taken such a dramatic decision. She answered very calmly that it was neither sudden nor dramatic and had been discussed over a long period with her colleagues and Party.

Some months previously, Nijalingappa, the President of Conress O, had hinted that if Indira Gandhi were suitably repentant, Congress O would consider re-admitting her. However, earlier attempts to patch up the quarrel had had no results, and one

117

presumes that his suggestion was conveyed to Indira without any positive result.

The Swatantra Party found an ally in one of Mrs Pandit's daughters who, in the *Indian Express*, attacked Indira Gandhi bitterly. This paper has a big circulation in Maharashtra, Gujarat, Madras and Andhra. A member of the Swatantra Party coined the phrase, 'Indira Hatao' or 'Get rid of Indira' to counter the slogan 'Garibi Hatao'. It was applauded at the cocktail parties of the rich and their hangers-on. But people mostly considered this descent to ridiculing personalities in bad taste, and it made little general impact.

Journalists asked Mrs Gandhi if she was sure she would be returned as Prime Minister and her reply was characteristic : 'I certainly hope so.' What more did she hope to gain by the election, since she had a majority in the present Parliament? Was it to enable her to carry out the measures in which she had so far failed? 'It is good to let the people express their approval or disapproval of what we propose to do. And in any case the Opposition as well as the press have been asking us to seek a mandate from the country, so now we have decided to take their advice.'

Mrs Gandhi had made it quite clear that the progress of socialism was her party's objective and if she were returned to power her party would have to deal with reactionary forces and such vested interests as were proving obstructive to the socio-economic programme. This would be the main plank on which she would fight her election battle.

Mrs Gandhi's opponents maintained that she was afraid to go to the polls after her budget, because it would contain proposals for heavy taxation. The budget would be put before Parliament in April 1971; hence the snap election. Even if this were true, she seemed prepared to stake the substantial majority she already had in the hope of gaining an even larger majority. It was a mystery to her critics. She had also made it absolutely clear that there would be no election 'understandings' with other parties. Congress R would contest each of the 520 seats on its own.

'The Constitution is there to protect the people's rights. Now, when there is a conflict between a few people and a mass of people, some way has to be found to resolve it. You just cannot say that we cannot do anything for the larger number of people. Some way has to be found. We want to find a democratic and constitutional way. . . . If the Constitution needs changing, then that has to be explored and ways found to change it. It is a matter which has to be gone into in some detail because of the view the Supreme Court has taken. But I want it to be clear that when we talk, we are not in favour of removing all the fundamental rights nor are we even against the right to property, but we believe in having a certain ceiling on property, whether urban or rural.' So Indira Gandhi said on the eve of the elections. She emphasized the inequality between the rich and the poor and the extent to which poverty prevailed in India; it must be understood that things could not be righted overnight. It was a long and hard process but if the people knew that an effort was being made to bring this about, even the poorest would have some hope that one day the goal might be reached.

How could she face an election, Mrs Gandhi was asked, with the rising unemployment that existed at the moment, or perhaps she had a plan to tackle this, which she would put to the electorate? Her master plan for most national decisions, said the Prime Minister, was the Five Year Plan which would increase the resources of the country and provide employment for many. Young people were being encouraged to try out various projects as well as the schemes for self-employment. There were concrete plans to provide employment for a minimum of 1,000 persons in each district. At least a start had been made; it was not just an election pledge.

From the New Year, 1971, Mrs Gandhi began her election campaign. She was standing for her seat at Rae Bareilly in Uttar Pradesh, where she was opposed by Raj Narain, a Jan Sangh (Hindu Communal) candidate who hoped to defeat India's Prime Minister on her home territory. He contested the seat fiercely. But Indira Gandhi had no doubts of her own success. When she first contested the elections in 1967, she had chosen Rae Bareilly, her husband's seat, instead of Phulpur which was her father's, and where Jawaharlal Nehru's daughter would be elected automatically. The identification with her husband and the fact that she had sought a mandate from the people on her own merits had, perhaps, added to her prestige in the district. The outcome did not, therefore, cause her much anxiety.

Indira Gandhi, nevertheless, put all her energies into the election campaign and for two months she toured every corner of India speaking in support of the Congress candidate in each area. Sometimes she would undertake as many as three plane journeys a day, working during the flights at the many files that still had to be dealt with. It was an amazing feat for a woman who for half her life had been considered frail of health, but who continued to protest that she was never too weak for work that had to be done. The pace she set for this election sometimes left her male colleagues gasping. They, too, were carrying on with their work as Ministers, taking long weekends to go to their own constituencies, and speaking also for the Lok-Sabha candidates in their States. But the Prime Minister was everywhere with her slogan of 'Garibi Hatao', making the rich feel selfconscious, perhaps even temporarily guilty. To the poor she brought hope; she told them of the measures that would be undertaken to ease their burden. She also warned them that they must not expect miracles but promised that they would certainly see changes. The Indian electorate is a conscious electorate. In the past they had helped to bring about independence and now they were prepared to help Indira Gandhi, in whom they had confidence, to better their conditions.

Election-time stories about party behaviour, which appear from nowhere in every democracy, flourished also in India. The Prime Minister's younger son had commandeered Government jeeps and planes for election purposes; Government resources were being used to finance Congress R's election campaign; commercial firms were paying heavily into the Prime Minister's election fund. Mrs Gandhi made no comment on such stories,

3 Indira Gandhi with her sons, Rajiv and Sanjoy

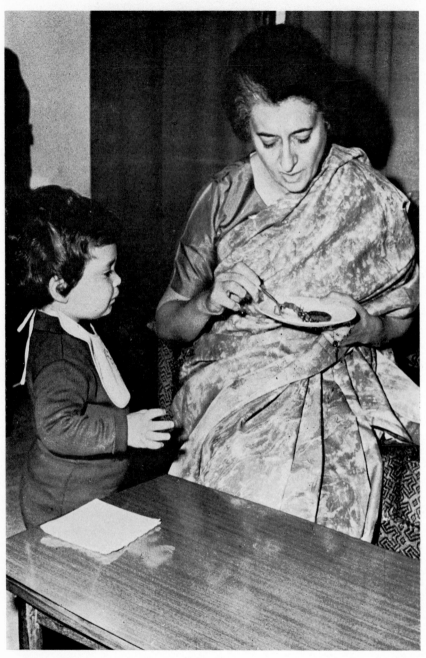

4 Indira Gandhi with her grandson, Rahul

since nobody was able or willing to produce concrete data.

Then came 10 March, the day of reckoning, and with it more stories of bribery and intimidation, but again no tangible evidence. The results came pouring in from all over India – it was a landslide victory for Congress R. In Delhi alone, previously held by the Jan Sangh, Congress R had wiped out the Jan Sangh. Indira Gandhi's Government had been returned with an over-whelming majority, unheard-of even in the time of her father. She had gained 90 per cent of the seats in Lok-Sabha. When she was asked if she were surprised, she smiled and replied: 'Of course not. Would I have gone into it if I had not been sure of my position? I knew the people of India, who understand me, would not fail me.'

Indira Gandhi's success had taken a great many people by surprise but her victory celebrations were memorable, with dancing in the streets of New Delhi and crowns of flowers brought to the Prime Minister to congratulate her. People will also remember the happiness in her face as she tried on one of the floral crowns. If on that day she had wanted to preserve the privacy of her own home, she could not have had the heart to turn such public joy away from her door, for these were the people who had reaffirmed their faith in her. If it was her day, it was also theirs.

The election results showed that, except for Morarji Desai, the Syndicate had lost heavily. Three woman MPs of Congress O, who had been foremost in their criticisms of and enmity towards the Prime Minister, had all lost their seats. Y. B. Chavan, Mrs Gandhi's Finance Minister, emerged from the election as the acknowledged leader of Maharashtra, having helped to bring the entire State to Congress R. Fears of his defection were now ruled out, as only a Congress R Central Government could maintain his ministerial position. Chavan's private ambition as a rival to Indira Gandhi would have to be set aside for a long time. The Prime Minister, in her turn, needed Chavan to keep the large State of Maharashtra.

The Government, back in power, took up its work where it had left off. On the other side of the West Bengal border, there had also been an election; Pakistan's Constituent Assembly, after twenty-five years of independence, was to frame its Constitution. The Awami League, under the leadership of Sheikh Mujibur Rahman, had won as big a victory in East Pakistan as Indira Gandhi had in India. This party and its leader wished to liberalize its relations with India and to develop East Pakistan (pre-independence East Bengal) for the benefit of the Bengalis. So far, East Pakistan had been exploited and developed largely to the advantage of non-Bengalis. The Awami League boasted liberal intellectuals and sound economists among its leaders. There seemed hope that with progressive governments in Pakistan and India, there might now be peace and reconstruction in the sub-continent.

Within a fortnight, however, the sound of guns was heard from beyond the East Pakistan border and military intelligence brought news which shattered all hopes of peace for Mrs Gandhi, as well as her plans to begin to banish poverty. From 25 March onwards, refugees from East Pakistan started their trek across the Indian border to safety. Empty-handed, hungry, but alive, they arrived on Indira Gandhi's doorstep. She now had to consider the basic needs of the destitute population of another country. Involved emotionally, strategically and financially, the Prime Minister had to admit that until the refugees at the border were able to go back, the Indian Government could not go ahead with any of its domestic plans.

This state of affairs continued for nine months until, at midnight on 2 December, Mrs Gandhi told the nation that India was faced with war against Pakistan. Pakistan, while Mrs Gandhi and her senior colleagues were out of New Delhi, had bombed Agra, Ambala, Amritsar, Pathankot, Srinagar, Avantipur, Uttarlai and Jodhpur. India had no option but to retaliate. The following day India was placed on a war footing and Indira Gandhi addressed a meeting of thousands in New Delhi, where her confidence, courage and faith in India's armed forces, and the justice of her cause, brought enthusiasm, hope and a nation-

wide solidarity. Indira Gandhi's personality convinced the people
that there could be only one outcome – victory. The religious and
superstitious muttered : 'It is the Mother Goddess herself – it is
Durga come to us in our hour of peril.' Thus began the Fourteen
Day War, the events of which are related in detail in Chapter
9.

Even Indira's opponents admitted their admiration for her
courage, diplomacy and skill in enabling India to act independently in this war. Her achievement in conquering critics and
making many friends during these difficult and troublesome days
was great.

On 15 December, two days before the war came to a successful close but when it was still at a critical stage, America's Seventh
Fleet sailed into the Indian Ocean and President Nixon stopped
all licences for the sale of arms to India. He also stepped up aid
to President Yahya Khan. Mrs Gandhi sent him this letter :

Dear Mr President,

I am writing at a moment of deep anguish at the unhappy
turn which the relations between our two countries have taken.

I am setting aside all pride, prejudice and passion and trying, as calmly as I can, to analyse once again the origins of the
tragedy which is being enacted.

There are moments in history when brooding tragedy and
its dark shadows can be lightened by recalling great moments
of the past. One such great moment which has inspired millions
of people to die for liberty was the Declaration of Independence by the United States of America. That Declaration
stated that whenever any form of Government becomes des-
tructive of man's inalienable rights to life, liberty and the
pursuit of happiness, it was the right of the people to alter or
abolish it.

All unprejudiced persons objectively surveying the grim
events in Bangladesh since March 25 have recognized the
revolt of 75 million people, a people who were forced to the
conclusion that neither their life, nor their liberty, to say
nothing of the possibility of the pursuit of happiness, was

available to them. The world press, radio and television have faithfully recorded the story. The most perceptive of American scholars who are knowledgeable about the affairs of this subcontinent revealed the anatomy of East Bengal's frustrations.

The tragic war, which is continuing, could have been averted if during the nine months prior to Pakistan's attack on us on December 3, the great leaders of the world had paid some attention to the fact of revolt, tried to see the reality of the situation and searched for a genuine basis for reconciliation. I wrote letters along these lines. I undertook a tour in quest of peace at a time when it was extremely difficult to leave the country in the hope of presenting to some of the leaders of the world the situation as I saw it. It was heartbreaking to find that while there was sympathy for the poor refugees, the disease itself was ignored.

War could also have been avoided if the power, influence and authority of all the States, and above all of the United States, had got Sheikh Mujibur Rahman released. Instead, we were told that a civilian administration was being installed. Everyone knows that this civilian administration was a farce; today the farce has turned into a tragedy.

Lip service was paid to the need for a political solution, but not a single worthwhile step was taken to bring this about. Instead, the rulers of West Pakistan went ahead, holding farcical elections to seats which had been arbitrarily declared vacant.

There was not even a whisper that anyone from the outside world had tried to have contact with Mujibur Rahman. Our earnest plea that Sheikh Mujibur Rahman should be released, or that, even if he were to be kept under detention, contact with him might be established, was not considered practical on the ground that the US could not urge policies which might lead to the overthrow of President Yahya Khan. While the United States recognized that Mujib was a core factor in the situation and that unquestionably in the long run Pakistan must acquiesce in the direction of greater autonomy for East Pakistan, arguments were advanced to demonstrate the fragility of the situation and of Yahya Khan's difficulty.

Mr President, may I ask you in all sincerity: Was the release of or even secret negotiations with a single human being, namely, Sheikh Mujibur Rahman, more disastrous than the waging of a war?

The fact of the matter is that the rulers of West Pakistan got away with the impression that they could do what they liked because no one, not even the United States, would choose to take a public position that while Pakistan's integrity was certainly sacrosanct, human rights and liberty were no less so and that there was a necessary inter-connection between the inviolability of States and the contentment of their people.

Mr President, despite the continued defiance by the rulers of Pakistan of the most elementary facts of life, we would still have tried our hardest to restrain the mounting pressure, as we had for nine long months, and war could have been prevented had the rulers of Pakistan not launched a massive attack on us by bombing our airfields in Amritsar, Pathankot, Srinagar, Avantipur, Uttarlai, Jodhpur, Ambala and Agra in the broad daylight on December 3, 1971 at a time when I was away in Calcutta, my colleague, the Defence Minister, was in Patna and was due to leave further for Bangalore in the South and another senior colleague of mine, the Finance Minister, was in Bombay. The fact that this initiative was taken at this particular time of our absence from the capital showed perfidious intentions. In the face of this, could we simply sit back trusting that the rulers of Pakistan or those who were advising them had peaceful, constructive and reasonable intent?

We are asked what we want. We seek nothing for ourselves. We do not want any territory of what was East Pakistan and now constitutes Bangladesh. We do not want any territory of West Pakistan. We do want lasting peace with Pakistan. But will Pakistan give up its ceaseless and yet pointless agitation of the last 24 years over Kashmir? Are they willing to give up their hate campaign and posture of perpetual hostility towards India? How many times in the last 24 years have my father and I offered a pact of non-aggression to Pakistan? It is a matter of recorded history that each time such offer was made, Pakistan rejected it out of hand.

We are deeply hurt by the innuendoes and insinuations that it was we who have precipitated the crisis and have in any

way thwarted the emergence of solutions. I do not really know
who is responsible for this calumny. During my visit to the
United States, United Kingdom, France, Germany, Austria
and Belgium, the point I emphasized, publicly as well as
privately, was the immediate need for a political settlement.
We waited nine months for it. When Dr Kissinger came in
August 1971, I had emphasized to him the importance of seeking an early political settlement. But we have not received,
even to this day, the barest framework of a settlement which
would take into account the facts as they are and not as we
imagine them to be.

Be that as it may, it is my earnest and sincere hope that with
all your knowledge and deep understanding of human affairs
you, as President of the United States and reflecting the will,
the aspirations and idealisms of the great American people,
will at least let me know where precisely we have gone wrong
before your representatives or spokesmen deal with us with
such harshness of language.

With regards and best wishes,

Yours sincerely,

Indira Gandhi.

The war was over before Christmas of 1971 and the newly
elected Government was back in business, with the Bangladesh
treaty to be worked out. The bulk of the Indian army had moved
out of Bangladesh and those that remained did so at the request
of the Bangladesh Government. Mujibur Rahman was alive and
had come back to Dacca (its capital) to take charge of affairs.
Once the mutual goodwill visits to and from Bangladesh were
over, Bangladesh was trying to come to terms with its own
problems.

During the Indian Prime Minister's visit, the joint communiqué issued by the two Prime Ministers incorporated within
it several items of great importance to the two countries:

(a) that the Indian Ocean area should be kept free of Great
Power rivalries and military competitors. They expressed their
opposition to the creation of land, air and naval bases by foreign

powers in the area. It was their conviction that this was the only way of ensuring the freedom of navigation and safety of the sea lanes in the Indian Ocean for trade and commerce;

(b) the establishment of a Joint Rivers Commission comprising experts of both countries, on a permanent basis, to carry out a comprehensive survey of the river systems shared by the two countries, formulate projects concerning both the countries in the fields of flood control and implement them. Experts were asked to study flood control and irrigation projects on the major river systems and examine the feasibility of linking the power grids of Bangladesh with the adjoining areas of India so that the water resources of the areas can be utilized on an equitable basis;

(c) India promised economic assistance including the supply of food grains and a continued supply so long as Bangladesh needed assistance;

(d) the revival of transit trade, which had ceased when Bengal was partitioned, and an agreement of border trade to be finalized at the end of March 1972 (which has been done);

(e) peaceful uses of nuclear energy – the knowledge to be shared by the two countries, and

(f) closer cultural ties in consideration of the close affinity between Bangladesh and West Bengal, the two Governments to undertake immediate discussions for the signing of a bilateral agreement on cultural, scientific and technological co-operation.

By these terms Bangladesh became one of India's principal import and export markets.

9

The Fourteen Day War

Indira Gandhi was a child of non-violence; her early years had been spent with family and friends, whose lives were dedicated to the cult of non-violence in the struggle for the freedom of their country. Thus her greatest time of trial began when it became clear that the Indian Army would have to enter into conflict, even though it was for the freedom of Bangladesh and to save the lives of millions of distressed people in that country. 'Perhaps it is the only just war in our time,' said a foreign observer.

On 26 March, 1971, the sub-continent of India reverberated with the piteous cries of the massacre of innocents. The ordinary people of East Pakistan woke up one morning to find the guns of their soldiers trained on them. Most of them did not even know what their supposed crime was.

After the electoral victory of the Awami League in East Pakistan, and its leader Sheikh Mujibur Rahman's determination to claim East Pakistan's just dues, the hostility of the people of West Pakistan, particularly of the party of Zulfiqur Ali Bhutto, which had also won a substantial victory in West Pakistan, became apparent to political observers in the sub-continent. In any event, the victorious Awami League was numerically superior to Bhutto's party. East Pakistan's democratic claims for a democratic constitution were being denied by the President of Pakistan. There was, in February 1971, no question of East Pakistan's breaking away.

By 28 March it became obvious that Pakistan was in the throes of a civil war and that in the eastern part a systematic annihilation, particularly of intellectuals, was taking place. Refugees had begun to trickle over the borders of West Bengal. Border forces on the Indian side could hardly force back poor wretches seeking to save their lives. The crisis was on India's doorstep; the heartbreaking plight of the people of East Pakistan captured the sympathy of most Indians and Mrs Gandhi was immediately faced with a number of pressing decisions.

India has a 75 million strong Muslim population, its largest minority group. Hindu fanatics could very well have endangered these lives by creating communal disharmony, tension and bloodshed. Mrs Gandhi's first care was for the safety of this minority, and to prevent internal crises from exacerbating what was already a difficult situation. There was general agreement, even from Jan Sangh, a powerful Hindu group, that to allow Indian Muslims to be used as political pawns at this time could be dangerous for India. The Prime Minister repeatedly emphasized: 'This is not a Hindu/Muslim problem. Atrocities have been inflicted on Hindus and Muslims alike. Bangladesh's problem now is to strengthen the country from within – fight enemies within boldly.'

Nevertheless, the pressure on Indira Gandhi to 'teach Pakistan a lesson once and for all' continued. Many people would have had her take over that part of Kashmir which Pakistan had retained west of the 1948 ceasefire line. She saw clearly that this would only aggravate the situation. Lok-Sabha, also, expressed its solidarity with the people of East Pakistan and tried to force the Prime Minister to decide on armed intervention.

The first diplomatic dilemma which Mrs Gandhi faced was that she must on no account be seen to be encouraging East Pakistan's bid for freedom; simultaneously she had to determine what was a correct stand to take in accordance with the general sentiments and sympathy which had overwhelmed the majority of the people of India. She shared the shock and the anguish which were sweeping through the country. However, she informed the Members of Parliament that, while she was fully aware of public opinion, she had to act within certain international norms which

set limits to any action India might take immediately. Indira
Gandhi said also that she wanted to make it quite clear that the
Government of India was aware of the significance of the situation, but it hoped that Members realized that the options before
the Government could not form the subject matter for public
debate at that moment.

A few months before the start of the killings in East Pakistan,
a plane belonging to Indian Airlines on a flight from Srinagar
(Kashmir) had been hijacked to Lahore and the hijackers, instead
of being punished, had been fêted all over West Pakistan by the
authorities. The passengers escaped unharmed, but the plane was
blown up. Protests and representations from the Government of
India had received no response from the Pakistan Government.
Since that time Pakistan air traffic had been banned from flying
over Indian territory. When the crisis in East Pakistan began,
Pakistan was forced to send arms and reinforcements by sea or via
Ceylon. Some Members of Parliament suggested a blockade by
the Indian Navy, but the Prime Minister calmly advised restraint.

Behind the scenes, Mrs Gandhi and her advisers made diplomatic approaches to Pakistan to try to curtail a massacre that was
fast assuming genocidal proportions. China condemned the
actions of the Awami League, but made no belligerent moves
along the North-East Frontier which would have embarrassed
India and prevented her from helping East Pakistan in any way.

In protest at their government's actions, two Pakistani diplo-
mats sought and were given asylum in New Delhi. They were
nationals of East Pakistan.

The refugees from East Pakistan were in the meantime piling
up on the borders of West Bengal and Assam. Inevitably this
made possible the infiltration of Pakistani agents, who also used
foreign relief agencies. There was no way of identifying them. In
the case of the foreign relief agencies, it was possible to be selec-
ive and to permit only those which were already known in India,
such as Oxfam, to operate. However, for reasons of security, a
great deal of valuable medical and financial aid had regretfully
to be refused.

Mrs Gandhi sent in the Indian Red Cross under the leadership of Padmaja Naidu, once Governor of West Bengal, who was well-liked and respected. Funds were provided from the Central Exchequer for relief work. Large sums were also collected from all over India and sent to the border for the same purpose.

Slowly, however, Mrs Gandhi became convinced that the correct political climate for the return of the refugees to their homes must be created. India could not afford to go on supporting people who did not belong within her borders. India was not an affluent nation. At the end of March 1971 Mrs Gandhi, through India's Permanent Representative at the UN, asked the Secretary General to advise restraint on the part of the Pakistan Government, to stop the slaughter in East Pakistan. The Secretary General, U Thant, was informed by Pakistan that this was an internal affair and did not come within the scope of the UN. Indira Gandhi then decided to make an all-out effort to enlist the support of the world powers, to persuade Pakistan to re-establish peace and harmony in East Pakistan.

In India the people, expecting action from the Indian Government, were becoming restive, particularly in the State of West Bengal, the severed twin of the State where the massacres were taking place. The severance had taken place during the partition of the sub-continent into India and Pakistan in 1947, when the predominantly Muslim part of the old British province of Bengal had elected to become part of Pakistan. The Border Commission had drawn an artificial boundary through the province, separating East and West Bengal. Since then, particularly in West Bengal, many people have dreamt of reunification, and the creation of a State independent of both India and Pakistan. In 1947, however, when East Bengal became East Pakistan, the arrangement was eagerly and voluntarily agreed by the people of the area, its chief architect being Mujibur Rahman, although the Bengalis had nothing in common but religion with the people of West Pakistan. Anxious to get rid of British overlordship and the rich Hindu landlords at one stroke, the overwhelming majority could not wait to become part of a Muslim state. New hopes, new ideas led them forward.

The disillusionment was not slow in coming. The people of East Pakistan had no language in common with those of West Pakistan; they did not eat the same food; the middle class Bengalis were cultured and educated, but they had allowed the Punjabis to replace their British overlords. All the Easterners' contacts lay across the border. They were now separated from their markets, which lay across the border, by Customs and military barriers. If anybody was making a living out of the bush lands of East Pakistan, it was the people of West Pakistan. In the past twenty-five years, discontent and resentment had gathered momentum. Groups and parties, communist-orientated, began to appear, particularly among the young, causing the older and more cautious politicians like Mujibur Rahman to consider the future anxiously. They gazed across the border for inspiration.

In West Bengal the Congress Party had fared badly. Its decline had begun with the indifference of Delhi when in 1948, after partition, refugees had come to Calcutta from East Pakistan. Under Congress rule, as the years went by, it seemed as if Delhi had written off West Bengal. The communists had always been active there and for the last ten years the State had been governed intermittently by an elected communist government. Three times the Central Government, at the insistence of the Congress Party in Bengal, had prorogued the State legislature and installed President's Rule, under which the Governor of the State rules autocratically, helped by the Civil Service and the military, in the name of the President of India.

Now, Mrs Gandhi was uneasy about affairs in West Bengal where, for over a year, the Maoists had been maintaining a reign of terror in spite of Government repression. Even the pro-Congress elements were becoming restive; remembering what had gone before, they feared the Central Government in Delhi would be no more prepared to take a definite stand for the Bengalis in East Pakistan, than it had considered the welfare of West Bengalis in the past. Communist influence in the State was all the while increasing. On the other hand, while the West Bengali malcontents could say that the Central Indian Government was indifferent and inefficient, there had never been a day when the fear of decimation had haunted the lives of the people of West Bengal. The evils across the border were a salutary lesson.

In other parts of India – particularly in the Punjab – Indira Gandhi was aware, not only of indifference to East Pakistan's affairs, but of disapproval of India's involvement. Voices reminded her that the population of East Pakistan had elected to separate from India, of the massacre of Hindus in various parts of East Pakistan during the partition.

From East Pakistan, meanwhile, came a constant stream of emissaries with appeals from the imprisoned Mujibur Rahman for military help and intervention.

For eight months Indira Gandhi took no action. She held her hand and watched with 'anguish and anger' the deliberate slaughter of a people. While the army systematically destroyed the intellectuals, students, professors and professional men and women, naval bombardment destroyed the economic bases of East Pakistan. According to a US journalist the destruction was extensive and included jute mills, tea factories, natural gas fields and all that could make East Pakistan self-sufficient again.

In May 1971, Mrs Gandhi informed the world powers that the future of the sub-continent of India was at stake. She sent her emissaries abroad to explain the complex and bitter struggle that had developed, with refugees on India's doorstep and massacre beyond India's border. Very few positive or helpful reactions resulted. Members of the Lok-Sabha were restless. Public interest and sympathy were all focused on the tragedy taking place in the neighbouring state. There was also some resentment that India had been forced into a position where millions of rupees were being drained out of her Central Exchequer to care for the refugees. On 29 May, Mrs Gandhi calmed the House by insisting that India could not send back the refugees until a political solution made it safe for them to go back. Approaches were made to Pakistan again and again, asking the Government to create a

climate of security for the return of the refugees and of peace for
the people who were still in East Pakistan. Mrs Gandhi stated
firmly that 'the refugees must ultimately go back and the international community will not be allowed to get away with ignoring
its responsibility to the refugees.' Pakistan and the rest of the
world shrugged off the problem; Pakistan admitted that it had
violated human rights in East Pakistan, but was not prepared to
make restitution or change its attitude. Once more the President
of Pakistan reiterated that the entire situation had been created
by the Indian Prime Minister.

Indira Gandhi's emissaries having returned from abroad with
empty hands, she was determined that she would go herself to
plead the cause of the people of East Pakistan, although she said :
'I do not go with a begging bowl.' She was determined to make
the leaders of the world powers understand the dangers to which
the sub-continent was being exposed. She was concerned more
with the preservation of democracy, basic human rights and
human dignity than with financial help. The dilemma had been
brought home to the people of India in a poignant manner; she
felt the rest of the world would also recognize it if she could put it
to them personally. She would explain that East Pakistan
(Bangladesh) had not wanted initially to secede from Pakistan,
but to claim its democratic rights.

Siddhartha Ray, a Bengali, was Minister of Education in the
Central Cabinet, a relatively light responsibility since education
was primarily the affair of each State and the Central Government had little overall power. In June 1971 he was put in charge
of refugee relief.

In the second half of July, President Yahya Khan of Pakistan
offered to meet Indira Gandhi, but she refused. She said that so
long as the democratically elected Prime Minister of Pakistan,
Mujibur Rahman, remained imprisoned as a 'traitor', she was
uninterested in meeting Yahya Khan. If he had anything to offer,
it should be offered to Mujib and what he accepted would be
good enough for her. There was otherwise no need or basis for
any conversation between the President of Pakistan and herself.

The United States continued its shipment of arms to Pakistan, and was otherwise silent. This distressed Mrs Gandhi considerably, especially as it was feared that the quantities were far larger than had been officially admitted. The attitude of the US Government, with its glossing over of the massacres in East Pakistan, brought about a definite crisis in Indo-US relations. Nevertheless, and despite the lack of warmth in her personal relationship with President Nixon, Mrs Gandhi was determined that she would make an appeal to the American people in person before she sought any military solution.

Outside India, the conflict in East Pakistan was being described as a Hindu-Muslim conflict. Indira Gandhi told foreign journalists that this analysis showed a complete misconception of the struggle. It was, on the contrary, an effort to annihilate the people of the eastern part of Pakistan – Muslims and Hindus alike were being destroyed. Destruction of the Bengali, particularly of the intelligentsia, was the aim of West Pakistan. It was an aim on a par with Hitler's dream of destroying world Jewry, and was accompanied by a parallel indifference (initially at least) on the part of the outside world. Indira Gandhi again appealed to Bangladesh to strengthen itself from within. This was a huge task, she knew, but the enemies within must be fought if their cause was to succeed.

The task before India was to remain united before the challenge forced upon her, while recognizing the realities of the situation. The Prime Minister reassured the people that the Government would do what was in the best interests of the country. The 'border security forces' were alert and alive to their responsibility. With regard to internal affairs, Indira Gandhi promised that while all Indians would have to endure stresses and hardship, she would see that no further burdens were added to those already carried by the lower income groups. She had hoped after the elections to be able to relieve some of the existing burdens, but the Bangladesh affair and the avalanche of refugees had compelled her to postpone her aims – but only temporarily.

The opposition parties saw in the crisis not a national disaster but an opportunity to attack Indira Gandhi for having failed to keep her election pledges. It was a chance for her enemies to make political capital out of the situation; they even alleged communal disharmony in order to embarrass the Prime Minister. She appealed to them not to sacrifice the national interest and the cause of justice and peace by making political issue out of the crisis. India, said Mrs Gandhi, was faced with a challenge of a magnitude very few countries had ever encountered. It had to be met with courage and it would be a great tragedy if obstacles were created by some of her own people and placed in the way of the policy dictated by the interests of the majority of the people of India.

The Soviet Union and Yugoslavia were the only countries who had so far affirmed their friendship with India and answered her appeal with an awareness of the tragic and dangerous situation in Pakistan. None of the Islamic countries, not even Egypt to whom India had constantly given support, were prepared to condemn West Pakistan's actions in its Eastern Province. Tunku Abdul Rahman, Prime Minister of Malaysia, said he did not wish to become involved.

Until August the world powers had by their silence condoned Pakistan's actions. Britain's response this time was more acceptable to India than it had been in 1965, although it was not positive; at least Britain had not tried to treat India and Pakistan as two naughty children. Alec Douglas-Home's awareness of the political situation was keener than that of the previous Labour administration. His attitude may have been affected by British press coverage of West Pakistan's actions in East Pakistan, which was condemnatory. Moreover, the British Council offices in Dacca had been attacked.

Indira's first significant international action was to conclude a Treaty of Peace, Friendship and Co-operation with the Soviet Union. This took diplomatic circles in New Delhi by surprise. Tsarapkyn, the Soviet Deputy Foreign Minister, came to Delhi in early August to prepare the way for Andrei Gromyko, the Foreign Minister. On 9 August, India's Minister for External

Affairs and Gromyko signed this historic treaty. The scope of the treaty was wide: it provided for mutual consultations, barred any arms aid by the Soviet Union to nations hostile to India and laid down safeguards against agression.

The question of non-alignment as a policy was brought up and the man who had perhaps worked more than anyone else to bring about the treaty, D. P. Dhar, adviser on policy-making to the Ministry of External Affairs, gave India's answer: her policy of non-alignment was not static in concept, nor was it sacrosanct. It should be discarded when it ceased to serve the interests of the country or needed to be adjusted to prevailing world conditions. Mrs Gandhi stated that India was not deviating from her non-alignment policy; the treaty was the continuation of a friendship that had existed with the Soviet Union since India's independence. Russia had helped India substantially in its industrial development. Even now India's fourth steel plant was being built by the Soviet Union: no foreign exchange was required, rupee payments were accepted and used to buy goods from India. The new treaty would bring regional peace and stability, in which of course the Soviet Union also had an interest, since her southern borders ran close to those of India and Pakistan. Non-alignment was in the melting-pot, some said. But Mrs Gandhi told a massive rally in New Delhi that India held her head high, and that she was no satellite of the Soviet Union.

By this treaty, Mrs Gandhi prevented the possibility of any agressive actions on the part of China to relieve pressures on Pakistan, and found herself a powerful ally. No longer did India stand completely alone. Should there be any fears of attack on the Soviet Union, the Soviet Union would not need India's military assistance, but neither could India be used as a jumping-off base for any power wanting to attack the Soviet Union. If at any time the USSR were to be menaced, India would also serve as a good economic base.

Kosygin went to Pakistan and tried to reason with Pakistan's President in an effort to avert a war on the sub-continent. He asked General Yahya Khan to create a political atmosphere in which it would not be necessary to split Pakistan in two. President Tito of Yugoslavia visited New Delhi and assured Mrs Gandhi of his country's solidarity with the cause of East Pakistan which India had sponsored.

Indira Gandhi was invited to visit Moscow in October 1971 for further consultations regarding the treaty recently signed between the two countries. She was received with great honour and accommodated in the Kremlin for the duration of her visit. Apart from the immediate question of Bangladesh, she wanted to discuss with the Russian leaders her future relations with China and further trade reciprocity programmes. Mrs Gandhi had said often enough : 'I want to live in peace with my neighbours,' but she wanted to find out what Moscow felt about India's resumption of friendly relations with China, which was progressing, however slowly and in spite of China's constant reiteration of friendliness towards Pakistan, even at the time of the Bangladesh crisis. Russia had been a friendly and helpful neighbour for a long time and her approval would be useful. This was given. Another achievement of the visit was a joint statement issued from Moscow, calling for a solution of the East Pakistan crisis, in keeping with its peoples' rights and stating that such a solution would ensure the speediest return of the refugees to their homeland. An Indo-Soviet Commission was also to be formed to review economic co-operation. Indira Gandhi returned to India before setting out for Europe and America.

With pressures on her increasing from all sides, Indira Gandhi left in November in an effort to convince the countries of the western world that there was still time for diplomatic intervention, particularly by the big powers, to stop genocide in Pakistan. Everywhere she went she emphasized that should she be refused help and co-operation to achieve a political solution peacefully, India was not afraid to take on the task alone. She did not spare herself in trying to allow the world powers time to decide on intervention.

All through October and November, Pakistani planes violated Indian air space, Indian towns on the borders with East Pakistan were bombed and civilians killed. The raids became bolder and border incidents were becoming more frequent. India had not so far retaliated, but continued to warn Pakistan that retaliation was not far off. Everybody waited for the Prime Minister's return from Europe.

In Europe, Mrs Gandhi received favourable reactions from Herr Willy Brandt in West Germany and from M. Pompidou in France. Willy Brandt offered to mediate with Pakistan. Mrs Gandhi told Herr Brandt that she was agreeable to his offer of mediation, but that whatever he proposed should satisfy the people of East Pakistan; this was the only solution she could accept. M. Pompidou called for a political solution to Bangladesh's problems. He assured Mrs Gandhi that France would try to help bring this about peacefully. France's cordial relations with China could perhaps help influence Pakistan, it was thought.

Indira Gandhi came to Britain and spoke to leaders of the Government and Opposition, explaining to them the realities of the situation. She also expressed her appreciation that Britain had not stopped the shipment of arms to India, but she urged them to use their influence with Pakistan to create a political atmosphere in East Pakistan that would make it secure for the people living there and for those returning from the borders of India. She made it quite clear that India had no wish for territorial gains or expansion. India wanted to live in peace and to carry on with its own economic development, but not at the expense of any other country. She appeared on television and spoke to the press.

At a luncheon given by the Foreign Press Association in London, Mrs Gandhi gave a press conference to journalists from all over the world, resident in London. She answered questions frankly, emphasizing again and again the realities of the situation in Bangladesh. She indicated that the refugees, each and every one, must return to their homeland. On being asked why she had allowed them in the first place to come to India, she replied: 'What would you have me do, get our border forces to shoot them down or send them back to be killed by the terror they had fled? I could not do either. But I am determined that the political

atmosphere will be cleared and that they shall go back.' Another
journalist said : 'Why are you so anxious not to take in these
refugees as part of your population. After all, you have 550
million people, what difference would another 10 million make?'

'The 550 million are Indians and are our responsibility. Why
should we take in even 10 million who are not our people? They
belong to another country. We can only try to make it possible
for them to live in peace and ensure that their lives are safe. It
is humiliating for them to live on the doorstep of India and be
objects of pity and charity.'

In America Mrs Gandhi's reception, although markedly less
enthusiastic than on her previous visit, was cordial enough and
she had several discussions with President Nixon. Just before she
left for the United States, the Indian Embassy in Washington had
informed her that America had imposed an embargo on the sale
of arms to Pakistan. The revoking of licences to export arms
worth 3.6 million dollars to Pakistan had removed a major
irritant for India. It was feared, however, that there were
several CENTO countries through whom arms could still flow
into Pakistan, just as aid had come through Turkey when the
World Bank had temporarily suspended aid to Pakistan.

After two days' consultations with the American President,
Mrs Gandhi summed them up frankly at the National Press Club
luncheon : 'I think the President knows now what we are thinking in India and I have a better appreciation of what the
American Government thinks in these matters – the President is
trying to find a way [for a political solution in Pakistan] but the
whole thing has got so entangled, it isn't easy.' But she was determined that having spoken to the man who controlled American
policy regarding the sub-continent, she would also tell the
American people her views. Mrs Gandhi spoke on the NBC television network and at the Woodrow Wilson Centre, in the
presence of General Westmoreland, Army Chief of Staff. At a
White House banquet she replied to the toast to India, emphasizing that while India was not unfriendly to Pakistan or China,
the genocide in India's neighbouring state could not be allowed

to continue. It was a situation fraught with danger for the entire sub-continent.

In New York, speaking at a special convention held in her honour at Columbia University, Mrs Gandhi said : 'India will not tolerate it if Pakistan tries to transfer its troubles to India, no matter whether Pakistan bought arms from China or any other country. There is a limit to India's endurance and India will not allow herself to be wrecked by Pakistan's actions.'

Indira Gandhi had hoped to persuade President Nixon to put pressure on President Yahya Khan of Pakistan to restore democracy in East Pakistan, but she came away with the conviction that President Nixon favoured Yahya Khan and would not interfere or influence him in any way.

Early in November, China indicated that although India was taking 'undue advantage' of the East Pakistan situation and China would stand by Pakistan, it was advisable to seek a reasonable settlement, and suggested that India-Pakistan talks towards a political solution would reduce tension on their borders. Zulfiqur Bhutto, then Foreign Minister of Pakistan, after his visit to China, although claiming to have been reassured by China, ruled out direct Chinese intervention in the event of any conflict with India.

When Mrs Gandhi returned from her trip abroad, she knew that the countdown had started. She was faced with major decisions. The problem of West Bengal was brought urgently to her attention by Siddhartha Ray, an ambitious young Bengali barrister and politician. Ray had direct access to the Prime Minister, as their grandfathers had been colleagues and leaders of the national movement in the 'twenties. He emphasized the depressed position of the Congress Party in Bengal and feared that unless something drastic was done to revive the spirits of the party workers, the 1972 elections in West Bengal would be another disaster for Congress. He himself had ideas as to how this revival might be achieved and, if Mrs Gandhi agreed to the action he suggested, he guaranteed that her party would sweep to victory in the next elections in West Bengal, and that there would be

peace, law and order. There would be no talk of cessation or of a
Bengal united with East Pakistan. There was, of course, a price.
Provided his plan was successful, he should be appointed Chief
Minister.

Ray pointed out to Mrs Gandhi the intensity of the West
Bengali population's bitterness because India had so far done
nothing in East Pakistan. He counselled that the moment for
armed intervention had arrived, together with recognition of
Bangladesh and the installation of Mujibur Rahman as Prime
Minister. More help to the guerrillas – the Mukti Bahini – was
to be the initial step and then the Indian armed forces should go
in. India had already lent a general to train the guerrillas for
several months. The impact of victory over Pakistan would go
far to reinstate Congress prestige in Bengal, especially as the communist parties were all against intervention. At this time neither
the Prime Minister nor the Army, Navy and Air Force Chiefs,
much less the people of India, had any doubts that they would be
victorious.

It was pointed out by Ray that if at this moment in time India
did not intervene in East Pakistan and secure Mujib's rule there,
power could easily pass into the hands of one or other of the
communist groups, most likely the Maoists, and then it would not
be long before communist influence spread to West Bengal, where
the Communist Party of India (Marxist-Leninist), as the Maoists
called themselves, was already popular as a movement. With a
grateful Mujib in the seat of power in Bangladesh, favourable
trade concessions could be secured and the strengthening of communist influence in both halves of Bengal could be averted.

Mrs Gandhi was well aware that Ray's analysis of the situation
was correct. If nothing concrete was done to create a stable
Bangladesh she was faced with the prospect of a dissident West
Bengal, leading ultimately to the imposition of President's Rule
– not a very democratic way of governing. The alternative was
to go ahead with armed intervention in East Pakistan, aiming at a
positive and decisive victory over Pakistan, and give Ray his head
as Chief Minister, with full powers of repression against all

rebellious elements. If as a result trade with Bangladesh was nego-
tiated and the Congress Party was re-established in West Bengal,
she would have subdued the one really troublesome State in the
Indian Union. Very soon, however, matters were taken out of
her hands.

Throughout the entire period of the East Pakistan affair,
during the worst days of turbulence, when the number of refugees
had swelled to 10 million, Mrs Gandhi did not lose her com-
posure. She continued to act in character, with strength and
restraint. She urged Pakistan to retrace its steps and show concern for the people of the eastern province; despite her sense of
urgency, she behaved as diplomatically as possible without indul-
ging in polemics or expressing rancour. President Yahya Khan,
on the other hand, day after day, showered blame on India and
India's Prime Minister. All his acts of aggression against his
people were explained away by him as the knavish tricks of the
Indian Prime Minister. Yahya Khan worked himself and the
people of West Pakistan into a frenzy. He appealed to the nations
of the world to condemn India's intrigues against Pakistan. In
spite of this provacation and the inevitable agitation over the
deteriorating situation, Mrs Gandhi advised her people to be
restrained and not to rush into thoughtless and hasty action.
During these days Indira Gandhi grew in stature in the eyes of
all her people, perhaps even of those who would have welcomed
a false move on her part. The majority of people supported her
and gave her the backing she needed.

War was the last thing Mrs Gandhi wanted; she had tried every
other means of solving the problem first. Some months earlier she
had said while outlining her economic and foreign policy: 'We
cannot afford a war every three years or so.' China in 1962,
Pakistan in 1965. West Bengal was an extremely sensitive State
and a focal point in any decisions Mrs Gandhi would take. Ray's
counsel, though drastic, seemed to show a way out of the impasse
of years – a reversal of the Congress Party's diminishing prestige.
She wanted Congress R to become established as a significant
party in West Bengal. She also saw that the futures of the two parts

of Bengal were now inevitably linked. It was more expediency
and realism than faith in Ray, a politician who until then had
had little impact on Bengal politics, that gave weight to his
counsels.

Pakistan's military regime, seeking to seize the initiative, on 3
December, 1971 sent in planes to attack cities on the north-west
borders of India and forced the 'child of non-violence' to the
point where war was inevitable. That night a state of emergency
was proclaimed throughout India by the President of India,
under guidance from the Prime Minister and her Council. This
was the second such declaration in the twenty-five year old
history of free India. The next day a Defence of India Bill was
introduced in Parliament to take effect immediately. Indira
Gandhi broadcast to the nation at midnight that day and told
the people : 'Pakistan has launched a full scale war on India. . . .
Agression must be met and the people of India will meet it with
fortitude and discipline and the utmost unity. Today the war on
Bangladesh has become war on India.' She inspired confidence in
the millions who listened to her and there was a general feeling
that it would not be a prolonged war.

Of the two big powers, Moscow was seriously concerned.
While offering no comments of its own, Soviet radio and *Pravda*
gave full publicity to Mrs Gandhi's words on the dangers of the
situation. The USA at once cancelled all remaining licences for
the sale of arms to India.

From 4 December onwards, since the Indian armed forces
were well prepared for attack, the campaign went well on all
fronts for India. The border forces, so long held back, were now
given orders to move in as and when necessary. The Indian Air
Force were ordered to smash Pakistan air power on all fronts.
In Bangladesh the IAF shot down nineteen Pakistani aircraft,
thus inflicting heavy blows on Pakistan's air strength in the east.
The Indian Army moved in on all sides, pushing the enemy back,
under an umbrella of air support.

On 6 December, the Indian Navy moved in to bombard and
destroy Karachi Port, while the Army made a big thrust into

Sind. In the east, Chittagong Port was bombed from the air. The Mukti Bahini carried on their fight in the cities, towns and villages. The Indian Navy was in full control of the Bay of Bengal bordering on Bangladesh. A Pakistani submarine had been sunk and several destroyers had been crippled in action.

Meanwhile, the Soviet Union gave her moral support to India and vetoed the US resolution for a cease-fire and the withdrawal of all troops on the sub-continent from each other's territory. The Soviet Union also warned other world powers against meddling in a war that was the sole concern of India and Pakistan. In India the Government made it quite clear that it would resist outside pressures and would continue to defend India's territorial integrity by repelling Pakistani aggressors.

In New Delhi the Lok-Sabha was forced to introduce new levies to back up defence efforts. The new taxation involved increased levies on imports (except food grains and books); an additional duty on iron and steel products, copper, zinc, aluminium and manufactured tobacco; an export duty on carpet backing and hessian and an increase on the excise duty on sacking; an increase in income tax payable by all companies including foreign companies. These levies were in addition to those already in existence through ordinances.

Mrs Gandhi's next move was the formal recognition of Bangladesh and she appealed to other countries to do the same. The main offensive in the west was broadened while the Indian forces in Bangladesh pressed on towards Dacca. The towns on the periphery were left partly to the Mukti Bahini with the Indian Army backing them. From the Indian border the refugees were beginning to trickle back with greater hope than they had ever had.

President Nixon, however, in his efforts to help General Yahya Khan and his military regime, criticized India severely. While admitting that India had grievances in relation to the crisis in East Pakistan, he stated that it was difficult for the US to understand India's recourse to military force to deal with the situation. A postscript to this statement was issued from the White House to the effect that President Nixon was not anti-Indian, but that he was 'just annoyed' with India for using military force against Pakistan before peaceful means had been exhausted. It would have been interesting at this point in time to have had access to the reports from his embassies in India and Pakistan.

The United Nations Assembly now called for a truce and cease-fire. India's reply was to reject this call. She reiterated that she had no desire to obtain territory in East or West Pakistan. Her troops would leave East Pakistan as soon as a political solution had been achieved.

While her victorious armies progressed on all sides, nevertheless it was a bitter Mrs Gandhi who addressed her people at a huge rally at Delhi University. She urged the nations standing on one side to make their final choice. India did not want to destroy Pakistan, but no outsider could help if Pakistan was bent on destroying herself. Mrs Gandhi commented that much had been done to strengthen Pakistan's army, but nothing to strengthen her people. She also suggested that some western powers could not bear to see India maintain her dignity and the high ideals of democracy and independence that she had cherished for so long.

The surrounded and defeated armies of Pakistan and their officers, knowing that only death awaited them if they obeyed orders from Rawalpindi, sent an SOS to U Thant, asking him to try to relieve the pressure on them. General Manckshaw, the Indian Army Commander, broadcast a message to the men of the Pakistan Army not to run away, but to surrender and they would be treated honourably as prisoners of war.

On 13 December, Indira Gandhi said again: 'We've no quarrel with the people of Pakistan and no desire to grab land.'

While the fight for Dacca, the capital, surrounded by three rivers over which engineers were working to build bridges destroyed by the Pakistani army, continued, the flagship of the American Seventh Fleet appeared in the Bay of Bengal. The Government of India saw this as an attempt to apply psychological pressure, and Indira Gandhi promptly gave the order that Dacca must be taken at the most in three days, even though this would mean using more men and would probably result in more casualties. On 14 December the Army Commander gave an ultimatum for surrender as its three-pronged attack began to tighten the noose around Dacca. Even then, the USA was thinking in terms of sending more arms to Pakistan out of some other countries' arms quota. The Russian Fleet, in the Vietnam area, also began to move towards the Indian Ocean. There were all the makings of a world conflagration if the two fleets clashed, but on 17 December the war ended.

The West-Pakistan-orientated administration had collapsed in Bangladesh by 15 December and its officials, including the puppet Civil Governor, had taken refuge with the Red Cross. Pakistan was now threatening its own military personnel because of their failure at sea and on land.

On 17 December, with the fall of Dacca to Indian troops, the war, which came to be known as the Fourteen Day War, was over and Dacca now became the capital of the 75 million people of free Bangladesh. It was indeed an historic day for its people who had fought so bravely. Much of the credit went to their guerillas, the Mukti Bahini. The contribution of the Indian Army was perhaps not adequately recognized. Even so, in Dacca, General Arora was lifted high in the arms of the people and showered with praise and gratitude. The opposing generals embraced each other and the officers fraternized. (This spontaneous action did not meet with the approval of authority. Older generals remarked that it was not in the interests of army discipline!)

In the west, while General Yahya Khan continued to say, 'War will continue,' Mrs Gandhi called for a unilateral ceasefire and the blackout was lifted throughout India. As she announced in Lok-Sabha that the war was over, she was greeted by thunderous cheers from all over the House. She also explained that the unilateral ceasefire on the Western Front was a recognition of the fulfilment of a mission. India had no extra-territorial objectives and her troops would leave Bangladesh as soon as the leaders of Bangladesh wanted it. But she had promised to send officers from the Indian Army to help Bangladesh reconstruct its own armed forces. The services of civilian officials had also been offered. Mrs Gandhi, however, asked the Army to remain vigilant on the western borders in case Pakistan did not observe the ceasefire now or later.

During this period Indira Gandhi's accolades came from many sides, but real appreciation came from the Army for her wisdom in leaving freedom of action to Army experts and listening to their advice during the campaign. General Arora, who had so satisfactorily concluded the campaign on the Eastern Front, had advised her if possible to wait until the winter months before undertaking any campaign, since at that time of year the mountain passes on the northern borders of India would be snowbound and intervention by the Chinese less likely. Mrs Gandhi had kept the peace until early December, when Pakistan took the matter out of her hands. To those who came into contact with her, she fulfilled her claim that she was 'a person doing a job'.

I O

Back to Work

Indira Gandhi's plans to improve the condition of the Indian people began to take effect at the beginning of 1972, in the aftermath of a major war. Although activity had had to be slowed down considerably in 1971, she had nevertheless been able to put through a great deal of legislation in 1971-72, and had initiated various schemes, with the ultimate aim of banishing poverty from India.

The Planning Commission, under the chairmanship of the Prime Minister, had been reconstituted, and was working under a young team of economists, scientists and executives recruited from the business world. C. Subramaniam had been appointed Minister for Planning. He was considered an intelligent, forward-looking and competent administrator. During the nine months of the Bangladesh crisis, the Planning Commission had continued with its research.

India is a country of approximately 700,000 villages and is primarily agricultural. Although the land is generally fertile and in some parts comparable with the soil of the Nile Delta, over-cultivation, lack of fertilizers and old-fashioned methods have been the outward signs of a general neglect of agriculture in India. Agriculture is not only India's main source of food supply but also the source of raw materials without which certain consumer industries could not function. Agriculture provides 50 per cent of the national income. Nevertheless, so far priority had been given to industry. Credit for farmers, until the present govern-

149

ment's action in nationalizing the big banks, was difficult to obtain, despite the fact that several credit institutions had been established in the rural areas. The rate of interest was never less than 9 per cent and to borrow Rs. 500 one had to pay various fees amounting to Rs. 55 which included interest, and was deducted in advance from the principal requested. Agriculture, until the change of emphasis, was receiving only 2.1 per cent of bank credits, the rest going to industry.

In 1963 the World Bank offered to increase its financial support to Indian agriculture through the UN Food and Agriculture Organization, but no advantage was taken of this offer. The Government seemed primarily concerned to build huge and prestigious industrial complexes, forgetting that without basic food requirements, nothing would be viable. The Life Insurance Corporation, in 1967, earned approximately Rs. 1,780 million from the rural areas, representing roughly 28 per cent of its total earnings, but its investment in agriculture was barely 3 per cent.

This had been the picture for many years, the situation culminating in 1966-67, when the scarcity in Bihar and Uttar Pradesh was so bad that it almost assumed famine proportions. Thousands suffered acute malnutrition, although there were no actual deaths from starvation.

In Mrs Gandhi's regime, food and agriculture now became a priority, and heavy industry consequently received a setback. For the first time perhaps, planners were made to realize that people had to be able to keep themselves alive before they could work in steel plants.

1969 and 1970 were good years for rainfall, resulting in food grain yields of 99.5 million tonnes and 105$\frac{1}{2}$ million tonnes respectively, in each case at least 5$\frac{1}{2}$ million tonnes above the yield of the previous year. Buffer stocks of grain were built up, enabling India not only to supply food grains to Bangladesh and to support its refugees, but to work towards ending the PL 480 aid programme from America. It was a good start to the 'Green Revolution', although it was essentially a wheat revolution; rice production was still low.

Providing land for the landless has been one of Mrs Gandhi's main contributions towards raising the standard of living of those at the base of the social structure. In an underdeveloped and over-populated country, land tends to be owned by the few, while the multitude are either landless or owners of small plots of land which are neither economic nor profitable. After independence and at the time of the introduction of the first Five Year Plan in 1951, feudalism was abolished but no ceiling on holdings was established and the feudal landlords were replaced by a *kulak* type of farmer. Indira Gandhi's fourth Five Year Plan established a limit to the amount of agricultural land one man might hold. After the Fourteen Day War, cultivable waste land was made available for distribution, and with it, protection from the pressures to which the helpless peasants had for centuries been subjected. In 1970, the Central Land Reforms Commission, composed of the Chief Ministers of the larger States, under the chairmanship of the Minister for Agriculture, undertook to provide guidance in the work of implementing the policy of providing land for the landless. Such implementation came within the jurisdiction of the individual States. It was vitally necessary to provide legislation which would remove traditional impediments to the growth of agricultural production. Exploitation and injustice within the agrarian system must be eliminated.

Considerable progress has been made in most States in giving legal rights to tenants and sub-tenants in respect of land they have been farming; more than 3 million tenants have acquired ownership in this way. Dispossession of tenants is being made more and more difficult. They cannot be completely dispossessed; some land has to be left to them. It was common for pressure to be exerted on tenants by large landowners to make them give up their rights to their land 'voluntarily'. Now, if anyone wishes voluntarily to relinquish his rights, his land is taken over by the Government and then re-allocated to another tenant farmer on the waiting list.

The problem of agricultural poverty is immense and cannot be solved merely by the redistribution of surplus land to the landless and the poor. Alongside this policy, the ancillary services vital for

more efficient agricultural production must be developed. To
this end, the rural areas were now helped with better credit
facilities; incentives such as tax relief were given for the young
and unemployed to get out into the country and help grow more
food. Aid also came in the form of fertilizers, pesticides and the
provision of irrigation. Tractor pools have made possible the
modernization of farming in some areas. The Rural Electrifica-
tion Corporation began its activities with a modest sanction of Rs.
700,000. The Central Government has set up development
agencies in forty-five districts to identify the needs and problems
of small farmers in these areas, to prepare appropriate programmes and implement them with the necessary ancillary
services and credit. In addition, the Government has also set up
thirty projects for marginal farmers and agricultural labourers.
These projects emphasize the provision of supplementary and
other employment opportunities and are primarily market based.

Special attention has been given to the location of cultivable
wasteland. So far 12 million acres of such land in large blocks of
250 acres, and about 4.5 million acres in smaller blocks have been
found. It is recommended that the resettlement of the landless
farmer should be carried out on the basis of co-operatives. Pilot
schemes are being planned in which some of the landless will be
given the opportunity to work on these new co-operatives. Co-
operatives have been in existence in India for many years, but
very few farmers benefited effectively from them. Now, small,
uneconomic holdings will be developed as co-operatives, so that
their needs and resources can be combined. Through the co-
operative banks which, since the nationalization of the larger
Indian commercial banks, have been functioning more on behalf
of the rural community than previously, fertilizers and pesticides
have been more readily available to farmers. In 1969-70 the
value of fertilizers distributed through the co-operatives amounted
to Rs. 262 million.

Help and encouragement for agricultural research is another
facet of Mrs Gandhi's agricultural policy. The Government of
India has decided to set up 500 Agro-Service Centres as pilot

projects. These centres will hire out tractors and other farm implements, set up workshops for the repair and maintenance of agricultural machinery and will also sell machine parts, lubricants, and so on.

Engineers will be assisted in the establishment of workshops for the repair, maintenance and hiring out of agricultural machinery such as tractors, drilling rigs, plant protection and irrigation equipment, together with such allied activities as the sale of spare parts and fuel. The Central Government has requested the State Governments and Agro-Industries Corporations to assist entrepreneurs in formulating suitable schemes and in securing loans from the financial institutions. The ceiling for loans from the State Bank of India for starting the centres has been fixed at Rs. 200,000. The Agro-Industries Corporations in different States, engaged in the supply of agricultural machinery and equipment through hire-purchase arrangements, have been requested to extend this facility and to reduce the initial deposit required.

India's first Nuclear Research Laboratory is being set up at the Indian Agricultural Research Institute, Pusa, New Delhi. The Laboratory aims to apply nuclear technology in the field of agriculture. The project has been financed by the Government of India and the United Nations Development Fund, which has provided assistance in the shape of equipment, expertise and training facilities. The Rockefeller Foundation is donating a nuclear magnetic resonance spectrometer, the lack of which had been a serious handicap for India's agro-scientists.

The 'atom-for-food' programme will be launched on three levels – selection of desirable varieties of mutants, stricter control over pests and better use of fertilizers. According to Dr P. N. Datta, Director of the Nuclear Laboratory Project, the purpose is not to produce more mutants but to screen mutants for better varieties, increasing the mutation frequency and eliminating neuro-toxins. It is here that nuclear technology can provide an added advantage over the cumbersome chemical methods employed so far, he says.

Prior to her re-election as Prime Minister, Indira Gandhi had had to leave undone a great deal of social legislation that was long overdue, including the abolition of one of the greatest discriminations in the social life of India. This was, of course, the continuance of the Indian princes with their privileges as super-citizens and their privy purses. Since their rights were incorporated in the Constitution, the relevant clauses had to be amended. Earlier, Mrs Gandhi had won Parliament's assent in the Lower House by the required two-thirds majority but lost it in the Upper House by one vote. Even the President's right to de-recognition had been challenged in the Supreme Court and the decision had gone against the Government. Mrs Gandhi now approached the amendments to the Constitution from another angle. The first amendment made the authority of Parliament, as representative of the people, supreme, so that any measure approved by both Houses of Parliament must automatically get the consent of the President. The next amendment strengthened the directives and principles incorporated within the Constitution by making them effective in relation to the distribution of the material resources of the community for the common good. The aim was to prevent the concentration of wealth and the means of production in the hands of a few. This amendment did not take away or curtail such rights as equality before law, certain rights regarding freedom of speech, property, etc. or the compulsory acquisition of property, and could not be questioned on the ground that it did not give effect to these principles. The phrase 'right to compensation' in the Constitution, was amended to 'amount payable not necessarily in cash'; it could now be in kind. There could be no litigation regarding the amount given or its inadequacy.

For the purposes of terminating the recognition which had been granted to rulers and abolishing privy purses and privileges, Article 353A was added to the Constitution. All other relevant clauses in the Constitution were suitably amended and Articles 291 and 362 removed from the Constitution by consent of both Houses of Parliament. A Bill was then introduced into Parliament and passed by both Houses on 1 December, 1971, for the de-recognition of the princes and the abolition of their privy purses and privileges. Lord Mountbatten criticized Indira Gandhi's action and expressed his sympathy with the princes, as part-architect of their position in independent India. He felt that she had flouted her father's memory 'because her father had been the man who had put the protection of the Indian princes' privileges into the Constitution in return for what the Indian princes had given up. He had done so with the express intention of preventing his successors from going back on the honourable arrangements made with the original Government. When the necessary two-thirds majority was not obtained in both Houses of Parliament then the President used the loophole in the Constitution to try to deprive all the princes of their privileges by "de-recognizing" the whole lot of them, whereas it was intended only for a single one who had committed an offence. The princes took this to the Supreme Court who upheld the legal position and after that I had hoped that Indira Gandhi would not feel it necessary to pursue the matter any further.'

As previously, some of the rulers again appealed to the Supreme Court with the plea that their fundamental rights had been affected. They lost their case and the Supreme Court ruled that no further such pleas would be entertained. It was alleged by some that the entire Bench of Judges had been appointed by the Government to carry out its behest. But what had actually happened was that the Government's Law Department had taken good care to consult the judges and obtain their views on the legality of the amendments to be brought into the Constitution. So the Government knew it was on firm ground when the Bill was carried through both Houses.

As the insurance companies had been forewarned, an act to nationalize all general insurance was introduced into Parliament on 20 September, 1972. The companies, although now Government Agencies, were given great freedom of action, while being fully responsible to the relevant Government department. There were no boards of directors as such, but boards of management whose members' salaries were related to those of Government employees. Certain sums were paid to former chairmen and board members, who considered these poor compensation for the business potential they had lost.

The Indian Government, while prepared to allow a mixed economy, was not prepared to entertain any business that had become uneconomical, unproductive or which was responsible for the dismissal of large numbers of personnel. This was the case with the Indian Iron & Steel Company at Burnpur, privately owned and once a well-established business. It was found in 1972 to be suffering heavy losses and this was affecting a large number of skilled technical staff. The Indian Government took over the enterprise, installed an overall custodian, but left its employees, under his authority, to run the business as their skill and experience dictated. This created a feeling of security in Burnpur, for the key positions in the firm were filled by well-qualified, young technicians who were aware of the problems besetting the company. They felt that the new situation had created a tremendous opportunity and a challenge.

Under the Fourth Plan, industry has been rejuvenated. When Mrs Gandhi had time, after the Bangladesh war, to attend to this area, she found that private enterprise was wearing a strangely self-satisfied air, for which on the surface there appeared to be no reason! Then she learned that the Planning Minister, C. Subramaniam, without previous consultation with the Prime Minister, had evolved a scheme in which State and Private industry should combine. Although the scheme was welcomed by industrialists and by some members of the Government, for whom the magic of private enterprise and the myth of its efficiency still lingered, Mrs Gandhi could not approve it, for such a scheme would be directly opposed to the Government's declared policy. Her first action was to transfer C. Subramaniam to the Ministry for Industrial Development as its Minister and to replace him by D. P. Dhar, a loyal member of her administration. Once again, in this matter, Mrs Gandhi had demonstrated her ruthlessness when she suspected a challenge to her authority on a subject of public concern.

In an address to the Federation of the Indian Chamber of Commerce and Industry, Mrs Gandhi underlined certain aspects of future industrial development:

> Your statement that the members of your Federation are in accord with the 'socio-economic objectives to which Government policies are directed' is very welcome. Also your recognition of the wider responsibilities of business which transcend the earning of profits to which I have often drawn attention.
>
> One of the most controversial subjects is that of what are now commonly known as monopoly houses. There is a certain advantage in size. Economies of scale can be reaped with advantage. On the other hand, size can also lead to exploitation. The Government attempt is to ensure benefit from economies of scale without the evil consequences which flow from the excessive concentration of the means of production and distribution in limited hands. One of the objectives of Government policy therefore has been and will continue to be the promotion of small scale and medium scale industries in areas of production where technology does not conflict with scales.
>
> For large industrial houses, the main scope for expansion exists in the 'core' and 'heavy investment' sectors where their contribution can be commensurate with their expertise and experience. However, even large houses cannot develop these sectors without substantial assistance from the public financial institutions. This is why we emphasize the importance of evolving a joint sector where the managerial ability of the private sector could be harnessed with support from financial institutions.
>
> Better industrial relations are as important as additional capital investment. Loss of output due to industrial strife reduces national income and the potential source of capital for the creation of additional jobs. The number of man-days lost in India is staggeringly out of proportion to the volume of our industrial output. It is a test of mangerial skill to create an atmosphere of solidarity between workers and managers. We can seek the co-operation of workers only if we can assure them of justice and fair play.

The working conditions and privileges of the old ICS cadre (mentioned in Chapter 7) remained to be brought into line with those of the younger IAS men and women. Indira Gandhi wanted the loyalty of the young IAS members but she had lost her battle to strip the ICS of their privileges. Most of them had between four and five years to serve before retirement; she therefore brought down the retirement age to 56 years. Undoubtedly some of them had great ability and integrity, and she decided that these people, once retired, could be re-employed in the administration departments of Government Agencies and Corporations. They would have their pensions, of course, but that was all – no privileges.

Industry had taken on a new look under the Fourth Plan. Encouragement was given to foreign investors but there were strict conditions whereby foreign enterprise could only function if the senior partner and collaborator were Indian; after taxation, profits could be remitted to the home country; such firms as could guarantee an export quota were given better chances for further expansion of their factories, and other ameliorative conditions such as lower internal excise duties. But penalties for failing to export the promised export quota were heavy. Of course, the primary industries remained the responsibility of the Government. Such foreign firms as had been in existence either pre-independence or at independence were asked to indianize more and more, but the new conditions were not enforced until and unless any anti-national behaviour became apparent. Most of the older foreign firms that remained and were encouraged were makers of vital equipment for India's industries. Others were encouraged to diversify their products. Old and new enterprises must work as Indian companies under Indian conditions and such restrictions as were necessary for the country's economic health.

Indian capitalism has so far not lagged behind foreign companies in syphoning-off profits. But capitalism in India is really mercantilism, except for the large and wealthy houses of Tata and Birla. With the ending of the Managing Agency system by Mrs Gandhi in 1970, aimed more at foreign business houses than at Indians, businesses like Tata's were inevitably affected. The Managing Agency system was perpetuated by the British – a kind of absentee landlordism in industry, whereby a company would station a managing director to keep the business going, who was responsible to the Board in Britain, and whose function it was to cream off the profits for the shareholders.

The House of Birla had fostered the independence movement financially and supported all Mahatma Gandhi's schemes. The boycott of foreign goods which was a nationwide movement helped to open the doors of the Indian textiles business to Indian capitalists, principal among whom was Birla. He kept his business within the family and when independence came began to diversify. Since 1947, Birla had tried all types of business, including motor cars. He had come late into the business world of India and knew of Nehru's socialist aims, and that he intended to build his economy on the primary resources of the country – coal and iron. He felt himself safe enough until the emergence of Nehru's daughter as an able politician, holding the allegiance of the people even more firmly than Nehru had. By shaking off the shackles of the Syndicate she had lost big business its good allies in Government. She was also set on a clearly marked road towards a socialist state. With her strength in Parliament she could do a great deal. So big businessmen such as Birla gave money to her National Defence Fund, to her election fund and anything that might halt her on the road which spelt problems for the Moguls of industry. However, they could not buy off Mrs Gandhi; she seemed determined on building up a socialist state and conquering poverty. But the Prime Minister is realistic as well as idealistic and, at a time when the country's economy had to be put on a stable basis, she was well aware that private enterprises such as the Houses of Tata, Birla and their smaller brethren had to exist. The export programme depended greatly on products from their mills and factories. As long as private enterprise paid its taxes and did not try to extend its empires at the expense of the little man, Indira Gandhi's Government would not apply the guillotine. Some day it might be necessary but there was no immediate prospect of this.

The Sarcar Committee, asked to report on big business and its practices, had wide terms of reference. Big business may not be in danger of extinction yet, but its methods will from time to time come under scrutiny. Industrial licensing is strictly controlled; there is a corporation tax and heavy personal taxation. Big business still flourishes and will tread a careful path to keep in business, whether it be guided by a super-westernized chairman or a shrewd Indian, versed in crafty political intrigue. For the Indian masses at the bottom of the heap, there is little to choose between them.

In industrial business circles it is said that while most of the routine business is handled by the bureaucrats in the Ministry, if there are any doubts in the Minister's mind, the case has to be referred to the Prime Minister for a final decision. It would appear that she keeps in touch with the functioning of each Government department. She is never unavailable and she tries to keep up with the problems facing her Ministers.

Through the Planning Commission, Mrs Gandhi launched the Housing Corporation for the lower income groups, its work being to encourage and finance the States to build housing estates within the rent range of the poorly-paid worker. A great deal depends on the State Governments and their efficiency to carry the project to a successful conclusion in which there will be no slums and less congestion. Even in countries with smaller populations and a higher standard of living, the complete eradication of slums has so far proved almost impossible, but Mrs Gandhi hopes that if the destitute are given better homes and a stake in them, they will prefer to live there rather than return to the primitive conditions they have endured for centuries.

Hand in hand with this programme, of course, goes social welfare and education. In the years 1947-50, there were 23 million children in school; today there are 83 million and the numbers are increasing every year. Despite the fears of members of India's small affluent segment that education of the masses will merely serve to swell the ranks of the educated unemployed, not to mention pushing their betters from their rightful positions, the

Government's objective remains education for all – at all levels. Unfortunately, since the country's financial resources are limited, the pace of education and the development of State institutions is of necessity slow.

In the field of social welfare, family planning has been one of the most important projects in which the Prime Minister has particularly interested herself. She has always been involved in social welfare work. But she maintains that the population of a country is an asset if one can feed them. At a press conference for foreign journalists she was asked what she was doing to cope with India's population explosion. She said : 'It is an obsession with people in the West. If we can feed our people, they are an asset. So our problem is really to grow more food and encourage them to grow their own food so that as a nation we can be self-sufficient.' Nevertheless, great emphasis is put on family planning, on contraceptives which are supplied free to women through clinics; sterilization for men is made easy and financial incentives are offered. There are sterilization clinics at easily accessible places, such as large railway stations. Propaganda vans tour the country and posters encouraging family planning are displayed in all the cities. The real problem is to convince a largely illiterate population of the need for contraceptives and sterilization, as well as to brush away any superstitions and fears associated with something quite unknown. A scientific solution is being brought to the people in their homes, but a convincing propaganda campaign has to precede it. Women, dedicated to their work for family planning, are helped and encouraged by doctors and the Government. The birth rate has fallen but not appreciably. Much still needs to be done. If there are problems requiring assistance and advice from the Prime Minister, she is always available for consultation and to organize such help as may be necessary.

11

Foreign Policy

'India's foreign policy,' Mrs Gandhi has said, 'is a projection of the values which we have cherished through the centuries as well as our current concern. We are not tied to the traditional concepts of a foreign policy designed to safeguard overseas possessions, investments, the carving out of spheres of influence and the erection of *cordons sanitaires*. We are not interested in exporting ideologies. Our first concern has been to prevent any erosion of our independence. Therefore we could not be camp followers of any power however rich or strong. . . . In the bipolar world which existed in the immediate post war era Jawaharlal Nehru refused to join either bloc. He decided to remain non-aligned as a means of safeguarding our independence and contributing to the maintenance of world peace. Non-alignment implied neither non-involvement nor neutrality. It was and is an assertion of our freedom of judgement and action. We have not hesitated to express our views on any major controversy or to support just causes.'

The most important development in India's foreign policy after the Fourteen Day War has been the achievement of talks with President Bhutto of Pakistan, representing a civilian government rather than the military junta. No other Prime Minister, not even Pandit Nehru, had been able to achieve this. President Bhutto, perhaps, realized that in defeat it was better to be gracious than to be belligerent. The future of the sub-continent hung on the ability of the three countries which had now emerged out of the old British-ruled India to co-operate. Their interdependence, if only they were able to recognize and utilize it, would lead to economic prosperity for all. Friction could only retard progress. Mrs Gandhi has aimed, since she came to power, to achieve friendship and at least a *détente* if not an *entente cordiale* between India and her neighbours. She is determined to follow up any leads that may come from her neighbours, and this includes China.

The first step towards starting a dialogue with Pakistan came in June 1972, when Mrs Gandhi and President Bhutto met in Simla and dealt with much that was outstanding since Pakistan's major defeat on the sub-continent. As confirmation that India had no desire for territorial gains, Mrs Gandhi proposed to return 5,600 square miles of Pakistan territory which had been taken by Indian forces in West Pakistan. This was a gesture of goodwill which not only the President of Pakistan but the rest of the world recognized as such. The question of the 90,000 prisoners of war was difficult, since these surrendered mostly in Bangladesh and, as such, came under the joint command of India and Bangladesh. Mrs Gandhi said early in 1972, and again later, that Pakistan's recognition of Bangladesh and the return of her civilian population would help to negotiate the return of Pakistani POWs.

The Simla Pact signed by the President of Pakistan and the Prime Minister of India can be regarded as the start of a new era in the relationship between the two countries. Jawaharlal Nehru had said, twenty years ago, that nothing can progress or prosper that is built on hatred and the builders of Pakistan and their allies had concentrated on hatred of India as their prime motive force. It had been in the interests of the major powers to see that the two countries never came together. With their supply of guns and arms they had battened on the mistrust that had grown up. America and China are both guilty in this respect; even the Soviet Union tried it, but soon saw that, ultimately, this was no way to exert influence upon India.

Mrs Gandhi, welcoming the President of Pakistan, said: 'This meeting is perhaps not easy for either of us. Yet I personally feel, and my country feels, confident that it should make a new beginning in our relationship. We welcome the trend of your broadcast, namely, to forget the past and look towards the future.' Mr Bhutto assured Mrs Gandhi that he was looking for peace and that Pakistan wanted a new beginning but past prejudices had to be overcome. This conference was unlike many international conferences in that agreement was reached that the Governments of the two countries were resolved to put an end to the conflict and confrontation that has existed for so long and marred what could have been a harmonious and friendly relationship and the establishment of a durable peace in the sub-continent. To achieve this purpose the two Governments agreed :

(i) That the principles and purposes of the Charter of the United Nations should govern the relations between the two countries.

(ii) That the two countries were resolved to settle their differences by peaceful means through bilateral negotiations' or by any other peaceful means mutually agreed upon between them. Pending the final settlement of any of the problems between the two countries, neither side should unilaterally alter the situation, and both should prevent the organization, assistance or encouragement of any acts detrimental to the maintenance of peaceful and harmonious relations.

(iii) That the pre-requisite for reconciliation, good neighbourliness and durable peace between them was a commitment by both countries to peaceful coexistence, respect for each other's territorial integrity and sovereignty and non-interference in each other's internal affairs, on the basis of equality and mutual benefit.

(iv) That the basic issues and causes of conflict which have bedevilled the relations between the two countries for the last twenty-five years should be resolved by peaceful means.

(v) That they should always respect each other's national unity, territorial integrity, political independence and sovereign equality.

(vi) That, in accordance with the Charter of the United

Nations, they would refrain from the threat or use of force against the territorial integrity or political independence of each other.

Both Governments were to take all steps within their power to prevent hostile propaganda directed against each other. Both countries would encourage the dissemination of such information as would promote the development of friendly relations between them.

In order progressively to restore and normalize relations between the two countries step by step, it was agreed that :

(i) Steps should be taken to resume communications – postal, telegraphic, sea, land, including border posts, and air links including over-flights.

(ii) Appropriate steps should be taken by each to promote travel facilities for the nationals of the other country.

(iii) Trade and co-operation in economic and agreed fields would be resumed as far as possible.

(iv) Exchange in the fields of science and culture would be promoted. In this connection, delegations from the two countries would meet from time to time to work out the necessary details.

In order to initiate the process of the establishment of durable peace, both the Governments agreed that :

(i) Indian and Pakistani forces should be withdrawn to their side of the international border.

(ii) In Jammu and Kashmir the line of control resulting from the ceasefire of 17 December, 1971, should be respected by both sides without prejudice to the recognized position of either side. Neither side should seek to alter it unilaterally irrespective of mutual differences and legal interpretations. Both sides further undertook to refrain from the threat or the use of force in violation of this line.

(iii) The withdrawals should commence upon entry into force of the Agreement and should be completed within a period of 30 days thereafter.

This Agreement would be subject to ratification by both countries in accordance with their respective constitutional procedures, and would come into force with effect from the date on which the Instruments of Ratification were exchanged.

Both Governments agreed that their respective Heads would meet again at a mutually convenient time in the future and that, in the meanwhile, the representatives of the two sides would meet to discuss further the modalities and arrangements for the establishment of durable peace and normalization of relations, including the questions of repatriation of prisoners of war and civilian internees, a final settlement of Jammu and Kashmir and the resumption of diplomatic relations.

Before leaving Simla, Zulfiqur Ali Bhutto said to Indira Gandhi : 'The Agreement we signed last night represents a breakthrough in our relations. I return home with firm conviction that we can embark on a new era of peace. If we implement the agreement with sincerity and goodwill we can give to our people the peace with honour and progress which we have not found for so long. Today we have the opportunity.'

Many in India questioned what had been immediately achieved by this agreement. Indira Gandhi's attitude was that for India to prosper there must be peace in the sub-continent. Physical links and cultural links made it both necessary and desirable that the two countries should reach a peaceful agreement. She saw progress in terms of co-operation and commerce between the three countries of the sub-continent, recognizing a parallel with the decision of Britain to join the European Community. She, also, in agreement with Bhutto, ruled out outside interference in their affairs by stating that all outstanding matters or conflicting views, as well as any that might arise later, would be settled by 'bilateral negotiations'. Thus, at one stroke, Mrs Gandhi lifted the question of Kashmir out of the United Nations agenda, and left it to be settled by discussions between India and Pakistan. People had always felt that it had been the diplomatic mistake of an idealistic Prime Minister, with belief in the comity of nations, helped not a little in his decisions by Lord Mountbatten, to refer the future of Kashmir to the UN in 1949. The UN observers were not welcomed, only tolerated. The Indian Army and the Indian people then felt that Pandit Nehru was perpetuating Pakistan's claim to Kashmir by referring the matter to UN and to a plebiscite. It was better to expel the Pakistani forces then and there from the small portion of the country they held. Mr Bhutto, on the other hand, has gone on record as saying that in 1948 Pakistan virtually lost the Kashmir war by leaving two-thirds of the State under Indian rule and agreeing to a ceasefire line.

To try to settle the future of Kashmir, India wanted Pakistan to respect the old ceasefire line of demarcation but there was a slight problem here: Pakistan's minor victory during the Fourteen Day War had been the capture of a small village – Thako Chek – 3 km. in area. Mrs Gandhi's army chiefs at their conference with General Tikka Khan of Pakistan stipulated that this village must be returned to India if the old line of demarcation was to be re-drawn. Mr Bhutto was prepared to exchange Thako Chek in return for a similar concession from Mrs Gandhi. Mrs Gandhi offered to return the occupied territory in Sind in the vicinity of Rajasthan and also in West Punjab. She hopes that the present line of demarcation will be respected by Pakistan and that there will be no more invasions of Indian territory.

It was also suggested that if there were no more attempts to coerce India over Kashmir, this control line might become the international border between India and Pakistan.

Mrs Gandhi's present agreement with Pakistan was considered a brilliant way of retrieving the position without destroying Bhutto's prestige with his people.

In December 1972, the implementation of the clauses of the agreement started with discussions about POWs and the return of Bangladesh civilians to their homes. Pakistan released 1,500 Indian POWs, and Bangladesh repatriated the Pakistan civilians. The fate of the 90,000 Pakistan POWs, whose atrocities against the people of Bangladesh were unquestioned, could not be equated with those of the Bangladesh civilians still being held in Pakistan. Bhutto explained to his Constituent Assembly that Bangladesh could not be reconquered and that it was reasonable to recognize this and enter into friendly relations with it. His party, however, would not agree to the recognition of Bangladesh, even though Bhutto explained that, ultimately, the ties of religion might bring them closer to each other.

Lord Mountbatten's view was that the Pakistani POWs had become political pawns through Bangladesh's attitude towards them and this made it difficult for Indira to deal fairly with the prisoners. 'I recognize this but I think it is a great pity that the situation now is such that the unfortunate Pakistani prisoners of war are suffering, when all they had done was to obey the orders of their superior officer.'

The POWs are being taken care of in India largely to save their lives from the wrath of the people of Bangladesh who wish to try them for their crimes against the people of Bangladesh and to execute them. Many people in India resent the fact that the POWs live in good conditions and are eating better than the average villager or agriculturist. These complaints, however, have not so far become too loud, mainly because of the people's faith in the wisdom of their Prime Minister.

Bhutto had no easy task to convince his people in Pakistan that he is only doing what he has to do and that he believes there is no choice before him. But the bile of hatred against India that has been nurtured for more than twenty-five years within the people of Pakistan by their leaders will be difficult to cure or even to dilute. The attack on members of the Indian High Commission in London on 20 February, 1973, by young Pakistanis armed with dummy but realistic guns, has the stamp of the Muslim holligans who used to terrorize civilians in the old British days, inspired by their politicians. The dead Pakistani youths, shot by British police, were treated as martyrs in Pakistan.

Mrs Gandhi has tried to give Mr Bhutto the opportunity to persuade his countrymen to adopt a rational outlook. So far he is the only one who is prepared to talk rather than fight, and the prospects for a lasting peace would clearly be damaged if he were to be overthrown in his own country. Therefore, when the so-called Chief Minister of 'Azad' (free) Kashmir acclaimed the final negotiations over the village of Thako Chek as a victory for

Pakistan, India allowed him his belief. Indira Gandhi is negotiating from a position of strength and she sees no need to dictate but recognizes the need to be firm. Her hopes rest on her ability to keep the dialogue moving.

With Bangladesh India has a Treaty of Friendship and Cooperation. Mrs Gandhi is fully aware that not all its population are warmly disposed towards India, nor do they fully recognize what India and her people have done for Bangladesh. The present government of Bangladesh, however, is fully conscious of its debt to Mrs Gandhi and that partnership with India will strengthen both countries. The Prime Minister of India knows that international relations do not depend on gratitude but on mutual need. Bangladesh realized that the situation could develop into a second Vietnam if the conflict were not quickly resolved; the possibility of interference from outside powers was certainly a real one. India realized, too, that helping her neighbour was also a step towards preserving her own integrity and borders from outside interference.

Mrs Gandhi expects Pakistan and Bangladesh to live with mutual respect and independence. While India will not rely on Bangladesh for total support at all times, it is better to have a potential ally on one side of her. It is good for India's trade, commerce and general development. To Bangladesh India can give much in the way of expertise. This has so far not only been denied to her, but by the decimation of her intellectuals she has lost much of her technical and other wealth. By language and culture Bangladesh is close to its twin, West Bengal, in India. They are bound to influence each other.

The last twenty-five years on the sub-continent and its traumatic experiences can be laid at the door of partition. Whom can one blame for it? The only party or person free from blame was Mahatma Gandhi who said quite openly that it was a bad idea and that partition would create many more problems than those that would emerge from living together in a united India. There is now again another chance for the sub-continent to try to live in peace and bring security to the people. 'There can be no progress where there is fear of a cold or hot war,' is the opinion of India's Prime Minister.

It has been Mrs Gandhi's first consideration not to allow India's independence to be whittled away in her relations with the big powers. In foreign policy she has pursued the idea of amity 'with no strings attached'. India's relations with her neighbours and near neighbours in Asia are, of course, also vital. Of these, relations with China are perhaps the most important. Mrs Gandhi would like to re-establish friendship with China through the five principles of co-existence in which Pandit Nehru believed, even though China has shown so much enmity towards India in the last ten years. If friendship between America and China has been shown to be possible, why not friendship between India and China? Mrs Gandhi has said quite frankly : 'I want to talk to China for the purpose of re-establishing good relations. But we cannot go on saying this over and over again if there is no response from the other side.' Nevertheless, it is reported that China has asked Britain to try to act as mediator; also, that Mrs Gandhi sounded out M. Pompidou to see if there was any prospect of France smoothing the way for talks with China. Her reason for this action is clear : with peace established in this area, India can go ahead with her own plans for development. Mrs Gandhi has gone on record as declaring that it is an oversimplification to say that China's intrusion into India in 1962 was merely over the border dispute. 'Simultaneous or subsequent developments – such as China's systematic support of Pakistan against India, her provocative criticisms of India for alleged subservience to the United States and later the Soviet Union, and her persistent though futile efforts to promote internal subversion – leave us no option but to infer that the border dispute was the outcome of a more complex policy which was aimed at undermining India's stability and at obstructing her rapid and orderly progress.'

After the cultural revolution in China, when life had settled down to a normal tempo, it seemed as if a new orientation of

Chinese policy regarding India was emerging : a thaw in China's attitude towards India was detectable. However, China's subsequent unqualified support for General Yahya Khan showed a hardening of her attitude towards India. Mrs Gandhi expresses the hope that some day China will appreciate that co-operative and friendly relations between India's 500 million people and China's 700 million could be mutually beneficial and must contribute towards stability in Asia. 'We are not engaged in any competition with China nor have we any hostile intentions,' she remarked with some irritation in answer to queries about her attitude to China.

China has to decide whether reconciliation with India would hamper its good relations with Pakistan. At present China seems to think so. India does not think that Indo-Soviet friendship is any bar to good relations with China. Perhaps China is thinking in terms of a future war against the Soviet Union, in which case both the USA and Pakistan would be valuable allies and India would not. If this were so, China would think hard before alienating Pakistan, unless it were possible to drive a wedge between India and the USSR.

Mrs Gandhi has declared that it is not necessary for Asian countries to continue as poor relations of the developed countries, or as mere suppliers of raw materials for manufactured goods which remain beyond the means of the populations of the so-called developing countries. The vast exhibition held last year in New Delhi, 'Asia 72', illustrated that the Asian countries have a role to play which is of the utmost importance to their development – participation in world trade. The trade fair emphasized the core of India's foreign policy – that Asian people should get to know each other's possibilities and potentials and evolve trade policies of mutual benefit. 'Indeed, neither growth, public welfare nor self-reliance is possible without an increase in our countries' capacity to export,' is how Mrs Gandhi expressed her ideas on Asian development. 'Unfortunately, prevailing conditions in international life and trade do not favour the growth of trade for developing countries. While the value and volume of world trade

have expanded in the last two decades, the share of the developing countries has steadily diminished. Urgent efforts are necessary
to arrest this trend, otherwise their share, which is as low as 17
per cent, might further decline, even though two-thirds of mankind live in these developing countries. . . . There is scope for
expansion of trade, economic co-operation and regional integra-
tion between our countries.'

'We do not deny the existence of Israel or that it should continue
to exist.' Mrs Gandhi sees the Arab-Israeli conflict as a nerve centre
from which a world conflict could be generated. The existence of
racialism between European Jews and Asian Jews seems incredible in a people whose immense sufferings have roused worldwide
sympathy through the ages. The experiences of Indian Jews who
went to their homeland when Israel was established and after a
period came back to India disillusioned, as well as those of
other coloured Jews who had similar experiences, have confirmed
the belief of people in India that Israel leans more to Europe than
Asia, of which it is a part. The intransigence and the violence of
the Arabs has never commended itself to India, nor the terrorist
activities of some Arab groups. The lack of co-operation and co-
ordination among the Arab countries has been a matter of regret
to India; as has been the Sheikhs' want of any consideration for
their poor.

Egypt, however, is quite a different matter. The friendship
between India and Egypt was established by Nasser, and Pandit
Nehru believed in Nasser's aim of relieving poverty. The friendship was also used by India as a defence against Pakistan. Indira
Gandhi, in an interview she gave to the senior editor of *Al-Ahram*
(Cairo) in March 1971, expressed her approval of the 'initiative
taken by the President of Egypt and the Arab world to try to
find a just solution to the Middle-Eastern conflict.' She felt that
such moves could provide a basis for a fair and enduring solution.
She also hoped for closer ties and understanding between India
and Egypt through trade and cultural contacts. 'I would like

Indians to study Arab writers and to be able to think in the original and not be content to understand the Arab world through intermediary "experts." ' She also explained that although the ex-Colonial countries were free, some of them were still tied to the old patterns of behaviour and it was necessary to break away from these. If, for instance, India's cotton industry needed expertise, instead of going to the USA, India should go to the UAR, whose cotton industry is highly developed.

Mrs Gandhi's foreign policy definitely includes friendship with Egypt and it does not exclude Israel. India is as mindful of the minority community of Palestinian Arabs in Israel and the necessity to safeguard their rights, as she is of her own Muslim and other minorities. It is, however, interesting that President Sadat neither commented on nor tried to dissuade Pakistan from carrying through its policy in Bangladesh, nor expressed any solidarity with India during the Fourteen Day War.

Among the larger countries, friendly relations with the USSR began with the aid and friendship given at the inception of India's independence. While there may have been patches of disagreement, the general trend has been one of friendship on both sides. Technical aid for which foreign exchange was not required flowed abundantly on the rupee payment system. The Russians made no attempt to increase their hegemony over the people of India and continued rather to cultivate the goodwill of her Government. The international objectives of India and the USSR regarding the maintenance of peace and the elimination of racialism and colonialism are similar.

Mrs Gandhi declares regarding the Soviet Union : 'In strictly bilateral terms also there has been a steady increase in the range and volume of our co-operation, economic, commercial and cultural – to our mutual advantage. . . . The Treaty of Peace, Friendship and Co-operation concluded last year (1971) grew logically from this expanding relationship. . . . There is nothing in the Treaty to which any reasonable person or government could take exception. It contains no secret clauses nor is it aimed against any country. . . . In the text of the Treaty itself there is explicit recognition and endorsement of India's policy of non-alignment.'

India's relationship with the USA has had its high tide, its shallows and quicksands. Since Mrs Gandhi does not believe in 'permanent estrangement' she is anxious that there should be a rapprochement between India and America, without India losing any of her freedom. She does not want to renew PL 480 aid to build up her buffer stocks but she is willing to continue to buy from the United States. 'The original misunderstanding had arisen because of our contacts with China, the Soviet Union and Eastern Europe. We find it difficult to understand why, when the US policy towards these countries changed, the resentment against us increased,' says Mrs Gandhi.

Edward O'Neill, former First Secretary and press attaché at the US Embassy in New Delhi, says: 'The yo-yo seems the most appropriate symbol to use in summarizing Indian-American relations during the 25 years of India's existence as an independent state.' He adds that five years ago US policy was one of all-out help for India's growth and development. 'Since we were pouring showers of dollars into India's development, $9.7 billion to the end of 1971, we appeared to be in earnest, but in the past one and a half years there have been changes.' These he attributes to the Nixon election.

The appointment of the liberal William P. Moynihan will perhaps see the start of a new and better relationship between India and the US, with greater understanding and fewer unrealistic expectations. It is, however, unfortunate, that on the day Moynihan presented his credentials to the Prime Minister, Washington announced the resumption of $15 million arms aid to Pakistan. O'Neill quotes a tough, realistic Indian editor: 'I don't believe there will ever again be the same kind of Indo-American relationship that once existed and I think that's a good thing. Our myths about each other have been destroyed. But I believe that we can look forward to a better relationship between the two countries, based not on our myths but our realities.' Another American scholar of Indian affairs, W. Norman Brown, comments: 'The recklessness of the American administration in its relations with the world's largest democracy – a natural ally of America – seems beyond explanation.'

Mrs Gandhi's attitude hardened over Vietnam. As she has said recently, if any European country had been bombed as North Vietnam has been by the USA, how long would the countries of Europe have tolerated it?

With Europe, India has had friendly relations, except perhaps with Portugal who could not reconcile herself to the loss of Goa, and could not take a lesson from the French who acted so wisely over their possessions in India. There are trading, commercial and cultural exchanges between India and France, and between India and both the Federal Republic of West Germany and the German Democratic Republic. In 1971, before the Fourteen Day War, Mrs Gandhi toured the countries of Europe pleading on behalf of Bangladesh for the great powers to intervene and effect a political solution. Her reception was cordial all over Western Europe. There was great understanding and sympathy for the cause she was sponsoring. With Eastern Europe there had always been and still exists understanding, trade and cultural contacts. With Yugoslavia and Marshal Tito Pandit Nehru had a special relationship which his daughter maintains.

Japan has held a special position and has for years been esteemed in India as a dynamic Asian country. India's co-operation with Japan in all aspects is growing. Japan is slowly replacing the need for European and American know-how in both industry and agriculture. Asians, Mrs Gandhi feels, share many problems 'which can be solved through co-operation among ourselves rather than merely through assistance from the outside which has tended to cause misunderstanding among us and which was motivated more by self-interest than by a genuine understanding of our needs.'

With Britain and the Commonwealth, India's relations are special in many ways. After independence both Britain and India were able to adjust their roles without rancour or even much debate. Edward Heath, Prime Minister of Great Britain, visited

India in January 1971 during Indira Gandhi's hectic election campaign. Then she said to him : 'Since our independence, Indo-British co-operation has expanded significantly. In some sectors of our economy our progress has been considerably helped by Britain's enlightened and understanding assistance. I hope that our association will be even more fruitful in the years to come and will help us to progress towards our goal of technological and industrial self-reliance. This gives a distinctive quality to Indo-British relations. We should like them to prosper and expand for the mutual benefit of our people and also for the larger cause of international amity and co-operation. There is so much on which we can build.'

Mrs Gandhi began to learn about Africa and the problems of the African peoples at the Bandung Conference of non-aligned nations under her father's leadership. Colonialism was entrenched in Africa, as much as, and even more than, in Asia. Certain aspects of western philosophy and culture had been bred into Africans more than was the case in India. The exploitation of Africa by various European countries had reached far greater proportions than it had in India. African attitudes are therefore more belligerent and more uncompromising than Indian. Africans had adopted Christianity as their religion and their education was moulded by missionaries. It was difficult for them to rid themselves of these influences, for they had really been deprived of their heritage. In their anger towards Asians in East Africa, who had been guilty of exploitation, though to a lesser extent, Africans could not see that they had been encouraged by the example and precept of the British rulers. These Asians had rejected their homeland and had opted for British nationality. They had become rich in East Africa but did not choose to plough back their profits into that country, nor did they wish to return to the land of their birth. They felt that by virtue of their wealth they were superior to Indians; they preferred to be the unwanted citizens of Britain. It is therefore only fair that India should feel no obligation towards these British nationals whatever their early origin or plight in Africa. Had these Indians asked for Indian nationality as their birthright, it is doubtful that India would have been deaf to this plea, in spite of its own growing population.

At Lusaka, in September 1970, at the conference of the non-aligned countries, Indira Gandhi expressed views on how the non-aligned countries of Asia and Africa should act. Non-alignment should be a vital policy, not to create a 'third world' as has been often said, but to enable the non-aligned countries to play their part in what is 'one world'. In her words: 'Here in Lusaka we can feel the ebb and flow of the continuing battle against the remnants of colonialism. . . . The revolution of our times is unfinished and the purpose of this conference is to draw up a clear programme of action to carry it forward. This is the challenge that the decade of the 'seventies places before the non-aligned countries. . . . The odds are tremendous. Let us not be deterred by cynics and the hostile propaganda of the powerful media of communications. There has been no lack of inquisitors who looked upon non-alignment as heresy and distorted its meaning. They said it would not work. But we can answer back in the famous words of Galileo – "And yet – it moves!" '

Asia and Africa contain a number of small, developing countries. They can progress and help their economies to grow by reliance on each other, and accept aid from the rich countries of the world without entering military alliances or blocs. All the countries on the two continents have been retarded by colonial rule, some more than others. They have become independent in many cases when the ruling colonial power merely abandoned its outward domination, hoping still to retain economic and political power. Such continuing influence was often backed up by centuries of cultural influence on the educated middle and upper classes, whose own venal attitudes made them an easy prey to the colonial rulers. Somebody once said of India : 'Beware that in your freedom you do not exchange the white *sahib* for the brown *sahib*.' India was lucky in her leadership and Indira Gandhi still fights the 'brown sahibs' who would continue in the path of their predecessors.

Indira Gandhi bases her foreign policy on friendship, anti-racialism and freedom from intimidation by the richer and more powerful countries of the world. The peoples of Asia and Africa have a difficult road to travel. There can be no security for India while even one country in Asia is menaced. Neighbourly inter-dependence and reliability, mutual assistance rather than depend-ence on the goodwill of the big and powerful countries and, above all, the preservation of sovereignty and independence – these are the essentials of Indian foreign policy. For India, Asian affairs have inevitable repercussions and Mrs Gandhi hopes that, while India extends amity to all countries, some day friendship on the sub-continent and with China will bring real stability to Asia.

I 2

Appraisal

On the twenty-fifth anniversary of India's independence, 15
August, 1972, Indira Gandhi spoke to her people over the radio :

At the moment of independence (1947), our energies turned
from the tension of struggle to the immediate problems of
partition and the vast new responsibilities which we had
assumed. That night Jawaharlal Nehru said in a mood of
prophecy 'the future is not one of ease or resting but of incessant
striving, so that we may fulfil the pledges that we have so often
taken.' A quarter of a century has since elapsed, during which
we have had our share of failure and success, tragedy and
triumph. And yet we can take pride in the undeniable fact
that despite the long sequence of challenges, we are today
stronger politically, economically and socially. Our national
unity, democracy, secularism and socialism remain strong and
firm.
  Our quest has been friendship with all, submission to none.
Our fight was not for ourselves alone but for all mankind. Nor
was it merely for political independence in its narrow sense.
We were determined to change the old order, to eradicate
poverty, to emancipate society from rigid stratification, evil
customs and superstition. . . . The greatness for which we strive
is not the arrogance of military power or the avarice of economic exploitation but is the true greatness of spirit which India
has cherished through the millennia.

Thus Indira Gandhi spoke of her hopes and ideas for the future for India.

Any evaluation of the present condition of India under Indira Gandhi's Government can only concern itself with the period from the end of the Indo-Pakistan War up to the present. Her earlier terms as Prime Minister could be called exploratory, for she was much occupied with seeking security of tenure in order to be able to achieve the measures she considered necessary for the evolution of a socialist state and economic stability.

In statecraft, one of Mrs Gandhi's greatest achievements has been to bring a younger age group into her Government. In finding younger people of ability in all fields from all parts of India, she has also tried to find the right places for them. Now there are many who would like her to bring in even younger people of promise, if necessary without the required experience. There are some who say she will never be able to fire the enthusiasm and imagination of the youth of her time as her father did; he was certainly the darling of his age. But his daughter is working in a different context, often fouled by frustration. This frustration she feels has led to all kinds of extremism – Left and Right. The Maoists of India are a case in point, she says, who think that the answer to all problems comes out of the barrel of a gun. They are reminiscent of the intellectual revolutionaries of the 1860s in Russia.

Indira Gandhi knows that chaos breeds chaos. In West Bengal, where communists and Maoists held sway, the situation has changed so radically under her regime that where there was a flight of capital from the State there is now a reversal of that process. Regrettably she has done this by allowing her Government to counter violence with violence. Police brutality and terror reign supreme. Requisitioning of gangsters by political parties has always existed, and unfortunately Indira Gandhi's Congress Party is no exception. Law and order have been re-established but it is the law and order of local dictators. Those who question or express a different view do so at the peril of their lives. The resulting stability is, however, good for business, which will mean employment for the educated. It is less good for what West Bengal has hitherto represented, for ardent nationalism, for the morale of the ordinary people, for art, music, literature. Indira Gandhi has understood better than her father did that there are certain Bengalis who can and will keep their fellow Bengalis down. She has exploited that awareness in order to achieve a temporary stability. All is peaceful now, but a bitterness still lies below the surface, and it will disappear only when her socialist state is achieved.

It is the little people, the masses, through whom revolutions are made. They returned Indira Gandhi to power, they believe in her, they love her; but how long will this continue if their sons are subjected to police brutality and to the strong-arm tactics of Congress politicians? They did not put her into power to make life safe for the middle classes. Mrs Gandhi has enormous reserves of popular goodwill to draw upon. She should employ her clever politicians with caution. Her own position and the state of the country call for the judgement of Solomon.

It is claimed that Uttar Pradesh needs the Prime Minister's attention, that it is suffering from dishonest politicians whose cupidity is fouling the affairs of one of the largest States in India. There is graft, there is political corruption, with politicians crossing the floor of the House for a price or favour, so that the people of the State do not know whom to trust or what to expect. Until Congress R's electoral victory, Uttar Pradesh was a stronghold of the present Opposition parties. Mrs Gandhi has quite a job ahead of her to clean up the affairs of her own home State. Strong-arm tactics may not be quite so readily tolerated in Uttar Pradesh as they have been in Bengal. She must first find a suitable Chief Minister. Whoever it may be, and however he or she may tackle the situation, the permitting of political parties to maintain private armies on their pay roll, to supplement the State police, should not be allowed to continue.

Indira Gandhi also has to deal with the activities of foreign agents whose plausibility very often deceives those in influential positions, including journalists who in their reporting express views that are often not in the interests of the country. The Central Intelligence Agency of the United States is among the most active and best informed on Indian politics. They have had a base in India since independence and a headquarters in New Delhi until Mrs Gandhi curtailed their activities through the various Foundations the Agency sponsored. Nevertheless, even now the CIA functions efficiently and foments anti-Indira Gandhi movements such as the cow slaughter agitation referred to previously. The CIA also tries to influence politicians through whom the Government might be brought down. CIA activities take various forms, all innocuous on the surface but which usually prove to conceal subversive possibilities. Mrs Gandhi and her Government have to exercise constant vigilance because the CIA sometimes works through other nations with whom Indians are in sympathy.

Opposition to Mrs Gandhi in Parliament is weak. In fact, even in her own party, there is nobody who can be considered a challenge to her. This was also said of her father, Pandit Nehru, but there is a difference in that he had certain weaknesses which rendered him vulnerable; his objectivity made him consider his opponent's point of view, which is an admirable quality in a writer but not in a politician. He became Prime Minister at a much later age than his daughter, after a lifetime spent in and out of gaol in the struggle for independence. It is said that the successful revolutionary is rarely a successful administrator. The circumstances in which his daughter rose to power were completely different. Indira Gandhi became Prime Minister when she was less than fifty years of age. She has the same integrity as her father, she has inherited his capacity for work and her courage on all occasions has amazed even her enemies. She is also farsighted and ruthless. Indira Gandhi intends to remain Prime Minister for as long as the people will have her. Time is on her side. There are those who declare that she is as great a manipulator as her father was, in placing her own people in key positions. Her father, it is said, achieved his ends more subtly by using others to accomplish what he wanted, but Indira apparently is seen to work towards her ends. She sees no need for hidden persuasion. In November 1972, there was the case of the election of Mrs Nandini Satpathi as Chief Minister of the State of Orissa. It was alleged by the people of that State, including members of Congress R, that the voting had been rigged, and that illiterate voters had been shown where to put their mark. Nevertheless, Mrs Satpathi was elected Chief Minister. She was summoned to New Delhi and returned, having satisfied the Prime Minister completely. Earlier she had held the portfolio of Minister of Information and Broadcasting where her manipulation of personnel in the Department appears to have inflicted a great deal of damage. Mrs Gandhi's loyalty to her seems inflexible. It is perhaps significant that Mrs Satpathi is reported to be a valued disciple of the 'Mother' at Pondicherry *Ashram,* and moves between New Delhi and Pondicherry with messages to and from the Prime Minister. Does Mrs Gandhi really believe that her strength and stability flow from her spiritual connection with the 'Mother'? This could be her one real weakness.

Since India's victory in the India-Pakistan War, Mrs Gandhi's position in India is virtually unchallenged. Many people dislike her policies or feel that her ideas of a socialist state menace their interests, but even such persons have pointed out that since 1000 AD when Mahmud of Ghazni invaded India, Hindus have been terrorized by Muslims. In the reign of the liberal Mogul emperor Akbar there was some relaxation. Since his death, there has been no abatement. The British played them off against the Hindus and this resulted in communal riots and killings. Indian lives and livelihoods suffered. By the defeat which Mrs Gandhi had the courage to cause her armed forces to inflict on Pakistan, she has forever now freed India from the fear of Muslim terror. She has brought a different dimension into the people's lives. She has re-created the Hindu empire and under her administration the Muslim minority living in India need fear no injustice or persecution. They are Indians. Millions of Indians believe this.

Indira Gandhi's first concern is the true establishment of secularism and complete eradication in any form of caste discrimination. Both these are implicit in the Constitution. She considers them as ailments that must be cured but her task is not easy. As she has said herself : 'I crush it in one area and it comes up in another.' She has said over and over again that what binds a people together is not race, caste, language or even religion, but one purpose and continuity of action to this end. But in India there are many isolationist tendencies, which have impeded the progress of Hindi towards becoming the national language. Most of the State languages are highly developed with their own literatures and cultures, whereas Hindi is of a much later development, yet two-thirds of the people of India speak it. Language problems are among Mrs Gandhi's foremost difficulties.

A personality cult has developed around Indira Gandhi which is not of her own seeking. She dislikes sycophancy but she would be more than human if she rejected admiration, even adulation. In December last year, there was an exhibition of the latest photographs of the Prime Minister, and it was held in what had once been her and her father's home, now the Jawaharlal Nehru Memorial. The exhibition was opened by the Minister of Planning, D. P. Dhar, by lighting a *deepa* (oil lamp) under a large head and shoulder portrait photograph of the Prime Minister. Such an act seems close to idolatry, for thus Hindus honour the images of their gods and goddesses. It was done as a tribute to Mrs Gandhi and it may have pleased her or, since she is a very practical person, it may have irritated her. It certainly indicated the beginning of a personality cult which could be as dangerous for her and all that she wants to do as any political opposition she might face. The Indian people are as vulnerable as any other and one cannot guarantee that their memory or their judgement will not be affected by politicians seeking to undermine Indira Gandhi's influence. The cult should be crushed before it is allowed to go further.

Having wiped out the existence of a princely order and all their hereditary privileges, it is of the utmost importance for Mrs Gandhi to impress on the people who have lived under feudal rule that the old laws have indeed given place to new ones, prevailing universally in the Union of India. Otherwise the Prime Minister's life could be plagued by the resurrection of ancient laws in various parts of India. She is faced with obsolete regional laws and State governments which find themselves unable to resolve a legal tangle which can lead to bloodshed and victimization. Innocent peasants, taught their lines by local politicians, can create a situation which has a touch of comic opera, in that the Prime Minister, having reduced the princelings to mere citizenship, suddenly finds a 'Mulki' or regional law creating seemingly insurmountable obstacles. Such a situation arose in Hyderabad, which was made part of the State of Andhra after independence. There the people invoked a law, passed by the Nizam (the ruling Prince of Hyderabad) in the 'thirties, in order to fight the emigration into his State of North Indian people. At present, Hyderabad having become part of Andhra State, Andhra politicians were monopolizing jobs for their own people at the expense of the local inhabitants. After a succession of bloody incidents, and an attempt by the Chief Minister to arrive at a political compromise between the two populations, the problem was referred to the Prime Minister who imposed an uneasy peace on the State by ruling that the 'Mulki' law would prevail for eight years. When the troubles still continued, she threatened to resign. This nobody wanted, so there is quiet on the surface, but it may be necessary finally for her to partition Andhra into two separate States, even though fragmentation would be economically harmful to both Andhra and Hyderabad.

The firm establishment of secularism and the avoidance of communal tension is absolutely necessary for economic stability. Religious strife, generally between Hindus and Muslims – it rarely involves other minority groups – has decreased, under Mrs Gandhi's determined efforts, to a minimum. If there is any upsurge, it is usually provoked by rabid Hindu groups or politicians to prevent Mrs Gandhi's plans for development yielding adequate results. Nevertheless, she does not intend to relax the vigilance which ensures the religious tolerance which India has cherished for centuries. According to the Constitution, any discrimination of caste, creed or sex is punishable by the law of the land and Indira Gandhi intends to enforce this rigidly.

Of caste, one can say that in two-thirds of India it has lost all its force except in the social sphere, for instance in the question of marriage. Upper class caste distinction, even in the social context, has disappeared but two questions still exist among the most liberal of people : Would you marry your son or daughter to a Harijan (Untouchable) or to a Muslim? Educated people, of whom there is a small minority, will accept either of these choices philosophically, but nobody likes it much. Others, who still wield a Victorian-type parental discipline, do not tolerate it, even if the suitor is wealthy and well placed. In rural areas the prospect of such a marriage has caused violence between families. Mrs Gandhi hopes for the day when such personal alliances will become normal.

In southern India and in the Deccan peninsula of central India, the caste system was always rigid. This area resisted Mahatma Gandhi in his campaign to secure at least temple entry for the untouchables, who were only allowed to worship their deity from the outer precincts of the temple. Mahatma Gandhi's tenacity achieved this; he changed their classification to 'Harijan' or heart of God. On the surface caste discrimination vanished; people paid lip service to the Great Man and the cause of freedom. Now, a quarter of a century later, one sometimes finds caste domination and persecution appearing like a case of rabies and, like rabies, it has to be eradicated with the utmost severity. There were cases in Andhra where Harijan villages were set on fire; in another area Harijans were falsely accused of stealing and were beaten up. The Government dealt with these and other cases with a heavy hand. The vigilance of Mrs Gandhi's civil servants and her determination to stamp out discrimination is the Harijans' safeguard. While incidents have occurred very infrequently in Madhya Pradesh and in Uttar Pradesh, it is in south India that caste discrimination still simmers.

One of the Prime Minister's continuing agricultural problems is that of irrigation. At present only 20 per cent of all agricultural land is adequately irrigated. Apart from the various ways and means adopted for the purpose of increasing food production, research is going on into methods of dry farming in which less water is required and the crops are of a kind able to survive rain failures. Rice yield is still below the nation's requirements but is increasing. Pulses and other seeds should be in adequate production for the needs of the nation in 1973/4. Wheat has done extremely well and farmers have produced surplus stocks.

As has been shown, one of Mrs Gandhi's greatest obstacles is the autonomy of each State with regard to its food supplies. It would require another major change in the Constitution to give the Central Government overriding powers to order the redistribution of surpluses. Mrs Gandhi is not willing to attempt this; she would rather build up her buffer stocks by buying grain from the States out of the Central Exchequer than alienate their Chief Ministers, upon whom she relies a great deal to keep her party in power. Mrs Gandhi's aim is to be able to give up foreign aid as soon as possible. US PL 480 aid for food grains has already been given up. Henceforth, she would prefer to be like other nations faced with scarcity, in the market to buy food grains if and when her own buffer stocks are exhausted and there is dire need in some part of India.

In spite of the depression and the vicissitudes which India has encountered, the structure of basic industries has been tenacious and has emerged strengthened. Heavy industry has gone ahead in an effort to be able to supply India's industrial complex with parts which hitherto had to be imported. Engineers trained in Britain, Germany, the USSR and the USA can now design steel plants, re-rolling mills and factories for the production of sophisticated goods. Three new steel plants are to be built, in Hospet in Goa, in Vishakhapatnam on the east coast and, from lignite, in Salem in Madras State. M. N. Dastur, consulting engineer, is producing the feasibility reports, until now handled by British, American or Russian experts. Very little of the equipment has to be imported, but since there is a shortage of steel, some steel will have to be imported.

If Sanjoy Gandhi's car, the Mathurin, goes into production, he will be India's first automobile designer and, while in terms of its price perhaps not quite the 'people's car', it will pioneer an indigenous motor car industry – a notable achievement.

India has put a great deal into atomic research for peaceful purposes. There are now two nuclear power stations, feeding the power grids in Rajasthan and Punjab.

The climate for foreign investment is favourable. India no longer has to seek such investment, since foreign business has come unsolicited. Britain is still the largest investor and India has opened an investment centre in London in order to deal with enquiries. In 1968 a British investor said : 'Find me someone who can make a decision and I will invest in an industrial venture in India.' Mrs Gandhi has facilitated decision-making, thus restoring confidence in India's stability. In a calm and favourable climate, certain guidelines are laid down for the benefit of foreign investors. India wants foreign investment but on her own terms : foreign investors are treated on a par with Indian investors, but it is necessary for the former to find Indian collaborators. This is an essential qualification. Normally, the policy is to allow minority foreign equity participation up to 40 per cent. Export orientated industries get preference and are welcomed.

In 1969 Indira Gandhi's Government set up the Foreign Investment Board as a single agency to deal with foreign investors and to avoid delay in decision-making. It works on the following alternative principles :

(a) foreign investment may be permitted with or without technical collaboration;

(b) only foreign technical collaboration may be permitted;

(c) no foreign collaboration – financial or technical – is considered necessary.

In 1947, 80 per cent of foreign capital was British; in 1968 only 40.5 per cent was British, 27.3 was American, 6.5 West German and 5.3 Japanese. Today, both Japan and West Germany have increased their investments, like many other countries which five years ago had only minor investments.

Small-scale industry is also benefiting from the feeling of stability, and from the loans now available from the nationalized banks. The small trader is able to expand and initiate new ventures. Several Indians who have been living in Great Britain for many years have been encouraged to go back, recommended by the Indian Investment Board in London, and invest their savings in small-scale industries. As Mrs Gandhi says, the villages are crying out for services of various kinds, and if the young, educated, unemployed Indian can be persuaded to leave urban areas, there is much to be done and earned in the rural areas. Finance for their projects would come from bank loans which are available for them to use.

Politically, many people consider Indira Gandhi to be a communist. The American administration seems to, but as she said : 'I dislike the word "contain" but if only people paused to think, I am containing communism in India. The Government cannot afford to move even the slightest bit to the Right because this will in no time begin a move on the part of the communists to take over, interpreting my actions as anti-people. I am no communist, as you know, but I do believe in trying to achieve a socialistic pattern of society in India.'

Indira Gandhi's country is a poor country; she continues to take steps to find food and employment for the people, a daunting task. Her talisman is that the people believe that nobody could do better. Although there is talk of corruption in high places, there is none around the Prime Minister herself. If donations are given to the Prime Minister's Defence Fund, there is no *quid pro quo*. Ministers and Secretaries have been dismissed at the slightest hint of irregularities. If there is corruption in government, it is likely to be found in the lower echelons, where salaries are inadequate.

In the last few years Mrs Gandhi has developed friendly relations with Canada, and Pierre Trudeau as Prime Minister has been co-operative. He invited Mrs Gandhi to visit him in June 1973, to discuss their international relationship, prior to the Commonwealth Prime Ministers' Conference, held in Ottawa in August 1973. Parliament is closed for the summer recess in India at that time, and the climate is at its worst. Indira Gandhi's first concern is food for India and so she accepted Trudeau's invitation. Her main purpose was to discuss a suitable arrangement for purchasing some of Canada's surplus wheat. At present Canada sells wheat to the United States which that country either gives as Aid or markets again. Recently Canada sold direct to the USSR and Mrs Gandhi feels that wheat might just as well be sold direct to India by Canada, instead of by way of the United States. If she has been able to make such an arrangement, her visit to Canada will not have been only a much-needed vacation.

Mr Edward Heath, Great Britain's Prime Minister, had also invited Indira Gandhi to London for a stop-over visit on her way back from the Commonwealth Prime Ministers' Conference. There is quite a good understanding between them and he appreciated that it would be difficult for her to be away from India for too long with so much work pending. Therefore, while she had to decline his invitation for a longer stay, they nevertheless arranged to meet and talk between flights. Indira Gandhi, despite her life-long affiliations with the Labour Party, finds it easier to talk frankly with the Tory Prime Minister, for she can neither forgive nor forget Harold Wilson's attitude to India in the 1965 India-Pakistan War.

Mrs Gandhi shows the utmost consideration to the people who work for her. After the India-Pakistan War, several *jawans* were decorated for bravery. The Prime Minister had something to say to each one of the considerable number at the investiture, pausing especially to speak with the widow of a *jawan* receiving the decoration posthumously. She had revived the rank of Field

Marshal for the General who contributed largely to the success of the War, thus also showing her appreciation of the achievement of the first Army Commander not to have trained at Sandhurst.

Indira Gandhi's childhood was lonely; after her mother's death her world was built round her father. Marriage she thought would bring her into a different world. But so many things including the condition of India, the uncertainty of everything in the independence struggle and the frictions between herself and her husband, flung her back into the loneliness in which her father was the only constant figure. With her aunts and cousins she had little in common. Her environment and her loneliness in youth taught her to contemplate and work things out for herself.

In her fifties, Indira Gandhi's personal life is untroubled and she is happy with her family, particularly since the arrival of her grandchildren. Politics is her career and she has reached the top. She feels quite secure in her Prime Minister's chair. Since she achieved power she has initiated many changes in government; she has valued the counsels of her colleagues. She has had the courage not to be overawed by her elders like Vijayalakshmi Pandit and Krishna Menon. She was not even afraid to hurt them. Efficiency and achievement came first. Her reactions are quick. She works hard, she seeks advice and at this period of her life she is at her best.

Some Suggestions for Further Reading

Abbas, K. A., *Indira Gandhi: Return of the Red Rose* (Bombay, 1966).

Hutheesing, Krishna Nehru, *We Nehrus* (New York, 1967).

———, *Dear to Behold* (London, 1969).

Moraes, Frank, *Jawaharlal Nehru* (New York, 1956).

Morris-Jones, W. H., *Government and Politics of India* (London, 1967).

Nehru, Jawaharlal, *Autobiography* (London, 1936).

———, *Glimpses of World History* (London, 1934-5).

———, *Bunch of Old Letters* (Bombay, 1958).

Rau, Chelapathi, *Indira Pryadarshini* (Delhi, 1966).

Index

Africa, 176, 177-8
Afro-Asian Conference, 55, 176
Agra, 7, 122, 125
agriculture, 94, 149, 151-3, 187
Akbar, Emperor, 183
Al-Ahram, 172
Allahabad, 7, 8, 19, 21, 24, 32, 33,
  37, 40, 41, 42, 43, 64, 72, 73, 74,
  98
All India Congress Committee
  (AICC), 104, 106
All India Congress Party, 41, 60-63,
  82
All India Radio, 77
Ambala, 122, 125
American Foundations, 103
Amritsar, 122, 125
Anand Bhawan, 19, 21, 23, 24, 27,
  36, 37, 40, 74
Andhra, 93, 118, 185, 186
Arc, Joan of, 28
Arora, General, 147
Arunalaya State, 115
Asia Foundation, 103
Assam, 115, 130
Attlee, Clement, 43, 49, 54
Australia, 94
Avantipur, 122, 125
Awami League, 122, 128, 130
Azad, Abul Kalam, 104

Badenweiler, 33, 34
Badminton School, 34
Bangladesh, 123, 125, 126, 127,
  128ff., 150, 156, 163, 167-9, 173,
  175
banks, 105, 109-111
Baroda, Gaekwar of, 114
Bay of Bengal, 70, 145, 146
Bengalis, 122, 132, 181
Bex, 34
Bhagvad Geeta, 16
Bharat Insurance Company, 48
Bhutan, 56, 57
Bhutto, Zulfiqur Ali, 128, 141, 162-8
Bihar, 92, 150
Birla, 158-9
Board of Film Censors, 77
Bombay, 41, 63
Bombay State, 63, 80
Border Commission, 131
Bowles, Chester, 90
Brahmins, 7, 22
Brandt, Willi, 139
British Council, 136
Brown, W. Norman, 174-5
Bulganin, 57
Burnpur, 156
Butler, Sir Harcourt, 25

Calcutta, 68, 89, 132

193